Creative Recovery

A Complete Addiction Treatment Program
That Uses Your Natural Creativity

Eric Maisel, PhD

Susan Raeburn, PhD

SHAMBHALA
Boston & London
2008

The information contained in this book is based on the personal and professional experiences of the authors. It is not intended as a substitute for consulting with your physician or other health-care provider. Shambhala Publications and the authors are not responsible for any adverse effects or consequences resulting directly or indirectly from the use of any of the suggestions discussed in this book. All matters pertaining to your individual health should be supervised by a health-care professional. The names, locations, and certain other identifying details of the clients mentioned in this book have been changed to protect their identity.

Shambhala Publications, Inc.
Horticultural Hall
300 Massachusetts Avenue
Boston, Massachusetts 02115
www.shambhala.com

9 8 7 6 5 4 3 2 1
First Edition
Printed in the United States of America

♻ This edition is printed on acid-free paper that meets the American National Standards Institute z39.48 Standard.
Distributed in the United States by Random House, Inc., and in Canada by Random House of Canada Ltd

Interior design and composition: Greta D. Sibley & Associates

Library of Congress Cataloging-in-Publication Data

Maisel, Eric, 1947–
Creative recovery: a complete addiction treatment program that uses your natural creativity / Eric Maisel, Susan Raeburn.—1st ed.
p.   cm.
Includes bibliographical references and index.
ISBN 978-1-59030-544-7 (pbk.: alk. paper)
1. Addicts—Rehabilitation. 2. Recovering addicts. 3. Creative thinking. 4. Creative ability. I. Raeburn, Susan. II. Title.
HV4998.M32 2008
616.86'03—DC22
2008016972

Contents

PART THREE

Living

Acknowledgments

Eric Maisel

First I would like to thank my coauthor, Dr. Susan Raeburn, for taking on this project, for her expert contributions, for her dedicated work on this book in the middle of a busy psychotherapy practice, and for her great good humor. Thanks, Susan! Second, I would like to thank our literary agent, Janet Rosen, for finding this book such an excellent home at Shambhala Publications. Third, I would like to thank Jennifer Brown, our editor at Shambhala, for cocreating this book by providing a steady vision, engaging in rigorous developmental and line editing, and demanding that we get things right.

For the rest, it is impossible to name all the individuals who have contributed to this book: all of my newsletter subscribers who responded to my call for information with stories of their challenges with and successes over addiction; all of my *Art Calendar* magazine readers who responded in a similarly helpful way; and all of my creativity coaching clients and workshop participants who, in our work together, have educated me about the addiction struggles that creators deal with on a regular basis.

Last, three words to my wife, Ann Mathesius Maisel, as we pass the milestone of our thirtieth anniversary: Thank you, love.

Susan Raeburn

My heartfelt thanks go first and foremost to Eric Maisel, my irrepressible friend and colleague, for his generous invitation to collaborate on this book. Working closely on the project deepened my long-standing experience of Eric as a smart, authentic, funny, emotionally mature, and thoroughly delightful person. I know I am not alone in considering him a force of nature. Thank you, Eric. Thanks to Janet Rosen, our agent, and Jennifer Brown, our editor, for their belief in the merit of our book and their perseverance in bringing it to life. Additional thanks, Jennifer, for your patient stewardship and vision for *Creative Recovery*.

Many people have contributed to this book by teaching me about creativity, courage, and the recovery process over the last twenty-five years. There is no easy way to credit adequately all of the individuals involved. Most simply, I want to express my thanks, admiration, and respect to my current and former private-practice clients in Berkeley, my former Stanford University Behavioral Medicine Clinic and Alcohol and Drug Treatment Center clients, and my past and present Kaiser Permanente clients. I also want to acknowledge my wonderful colleagues at Stanford University Medical Center during my tenure there (1983–1992) and at the Kaiser Permanente Chemical Dependency Services program in Walnut Creek, California, where I have worked since 1992. Colleagues from other professional communities such as the Performing Arts Medicine Association and the Society for the Advancement of Sexual Health (SASH) have also enriched my practice.

Perhaps my greatest lessons about addiction, recovery, and creativity have been from family members and friends. Some embraced recovery successfully and some did not. I am grateful daily for my family and friends who are alive and in recovery from their addictions. I remain sad every day for those I have lost: Kim, Thomas, Matthew, Christopher. All have taught me about suffering, compassion, and gratitude.

Thanks to my parents, Boyd Raeburn and Ginnie Powell, for sharing their lived creativity and gorgeous music, and to my brother, Bruce Boyd Raeburn, for companionship in the pursuit of integrating a love for music with academic pursuits. Last but not least, I thank my multitalented husband, Bill Delaney, for his kindness and helpfulness while I was working on this project and for being my greatest teacher of all about recovery and healing through love.

Creative Recovery

Introducing Creative Recovery

> There is no more cocaine. I check the wrappers, but they have been licked clean sometime in the night. My nose is bleeding now, the small sores cracked open by my puking. In four hours I have an interview on national radio and in six hours with a national newspaper. I close my eyes, not to sleep, but to lie in the dark of my body.
>
> —Patrick Lane, Canadian poet

The short story "The Bound Man," by the German author Ilse Aichinger, is a beautiful piece in the existential tradition. It goes as follows: A man awakens one morning to find himself inexplicably bound by rope. Instead of removing the rope at his first opportunity, as we might expect him to do, he decides to remain bound and to become a circus attraction, turning his accidental bondage into his trademark work. How strange! Why would a person happily accept such bondage? It is similar to the question that Franz Kafka poses in "The Hunger Artist," where a man who also chooses to become a circus attraction starves himself to death because he can't find food that interests him. These authors are asking variations of the following vital question: "Why do people carelessly, inexplicably, and even happily do things that harm them so much?"

Addiction is the same kind of bondage. Addicts cling to their addictions, and not for anything can you pry them away from their alcohol, cocaine, tobacco, Internet surfing, video-game playing, overeating, shopping, or sexual escapades. Tell them that they are dying: no matter. Tell them that they are wasting half of their life in front of a computer screen or in the aisles of department stores: no matter. Remind them that they can't have love or a real life if they use sex as a drug: no matter. Point out that their liver is already not functioning, that their nasal lining is already perforated, or that their lungs are already black: no matter. What you experience as you talk to an addicted individual is that he or she is completely indifferent to your good arguments.

Creative people fall squarely into the category of people at high risk for addiction—people who accept that happy bondage. This connection between creativity and addiction isn't a new one; the struggling artist is a character we're familiar with. But this connection isn't just romantic mythology—creative people are more prone than their peers to succumb to the lure of an addiction. And because creativity manifests itself in many ways, you don't have to be a professional artist to run extra risks for addiction. Whether you are a Sunday painter or world famous, someone who doesn't know what you want to create or someone who knows exactly what you want to create—if you have a felt sense that creativity matters to you, then you run added risks for addiction.

This book is an exploration of this relationship between addiction and creativity on a very practical level. We will explore the many reasons why as a creative person you are at greater risk for addiction, and we'll also offer steps toward recovery that use your creative nature in the service of your recovery. Along the way, introspective questions and creative exercises will be presented to help you explore your own recovery process further.

Since creativity can mean different things to different people, for the purposes of this book, we would like to offer a definition. We picture you in the following way—and this will amount to our complete description of the creative personality: we picture you as a sensitive, intelligent, thoughtful, ethically responsible person with a deep desire to actualize your potential; someone who responds to beauty and is interested in beauty; a person with a strong sense of individuality who nevertheless needs to make more-than-just-me connections; someone who would love to live an artful, art-filled, and possibly art-committed life that feels rich and authentic.

You may put your creative energies and creative efforts into music, painting, or sculpture, or into scientific research, your legal or clinical practice, or even your political or social activism. Maybe you don't know where to put your creative energies and efforts, and maybe you feel stymied by your inability to choose. Maybe you put them into so many different places that you feel scattered and unsatisfied. In whatever ways you manifest your creative nature, and whether or not you have found the way to manifest that nature successfully, you feel it pulsing in your being. If you see yourself in this description, you are at greater risk for an addiction. That is why we wanted to write this book, to speak directly to you.

YOUR CREATIVE-RECOVERY JOURNAL

Throughout *Creative Recovery* we want to pose some large questions that, because you are a creative person, we hope you will enjoy sinking your teeth into. We think that you'll learn a great deal from these self-investigations, so we encourage you to start a creative-recovery journal where you record your answers (and anything else connected with your recovery, including your responses to our exercises). To start, take the time to assess your risk of addiction by virtue of your creative nature.

ARE YOU AT GREATER RISK?

Answer each of the following questions *yes* or *no*.

1. Are you prone to boredom?
2. Do you prefer to do things your own way?
3. Are you eager to manifest your potential?
4. Do you feel under some pressure to make something of your life?
5. Do you feel empty if you aren't doing something interesting or exciting?
6. Do you dislike wasting time?
7. Have you ever fallen in love with a piece of music or a book?
8. Are you curious about how things work, including how the universe works?
9. Do you get frustrated when you see things done poorly or incorrectly?
10. Do you find yourself in opposition to some elements of your culture or your society?
11. Do you look for ways to improve systems or methods at work?
12. Do you change your mind on the basis of new information?
13. Do you feel that you sometimes have quite good ideas and quite interesting things to say?
14. Do you see yourself as more of a lone wolf than an ant in an ant colony?
15. Do you experience the passing of time as a kind of pressure?

If you answered *yes* to even one of these questions, you may be at greater risk for an addiction. Simply by virtue of seeing yourself as an individual with potential, as someone who questions life, who is interested in things being done right, and who gets bored when your mind isn't occupied, your addiction risks may be increased.

As we proceed, you'll also hear many stories, the majority of them from Susan's clinical practice. All creative persons have their own stories, both with respect to how they manifest or fail to manifest their creative nature and how they deal with or fail to deal with their addictive tendencies. Each story offers a different perspective on the recovery process. Here is a brief vignette that underscores some of the themes we'll be introducing. Debbie, a painter, explained:

I've always enjoyed creative activities. I fiddled with arts and crafts, I loved dance and music, and I've been a journal keeper my whole life. When I was young I wanted to be some kind of musician or artist, and I pursued that career choice by doing sex, drugs, and rock and roll. In my early twenties I used to do what I called dropping your soul onstage. I identified with Billie Holiday, Sylvia Plath, Jim Morrison, Janis Joplin, Kurt Cobain, and Jimi Hendrix, and I would get drunk and high to perform, which completely changed my personality. All the wildness trapped inside my introverted nature would spill out. I was not a pretty drunk, and the consequences got to be way too much. I had my stomach pumped out from drugs and almost died more than once.

When I first went to twelve-step meetings, I wasn't interested. I went to a few Alcoholics Anonymous meetings, but I wanted something easier than that, a magic pill or something. Years later, in the middle of a custody dispute, the social worker in charge of the case strongly advised me to go to Al-Anon. Al-Anon reexposed me to the twelve steps, and I started to look at my alcohol and drug use. By then I had enough negative consequences, guilt, and pain, and I didn't want to live like that anymore. During that following spring I made a foot painting: I painted the bottoms of my feet and incorporated my footprints into the painting. That piece was included in my first show in 2001. It is bright, playful, and full of joy, maybe reflecting the hope and relief that come after we get through' ninety days of sobriety.

I relapsed with marijuana, not alcohol, kept going to meetings the whole time I relapsed, and was able to get clean and sober again around Easter of 2002. I added Narcotics Anonymous meetings to my program around March of 2003, and I continue to go to NA meetings to this day. Creativity alone won't keep me clean and sober, but I've been able to use my creativity in the recovery process. I had to learn to separate art relaxation, which I now do in my morning and evening art practice, from professional artist goals, and I never forget that relapse is lurking in a corner. I attend at least one meeting a week of AA, NA, and Al-Anon, I do my art, and I keep my fingers crossed.

Just as Debbie was able to use her creativity in service of her recovery, so can you. We hope that this book presents information and ideas to get you started on your own creative recovery. We don't expect this to be easy, and we don't expect you to disregard traditional recovery methods, but we do hope that by acknowledging and embracing your creative nature you'll find a path to recovery that works for you.

YOUR CREATIVE-RECOVERY JOURNAL

1. Why should your creative nature promote addiction?
2. How can your creative nature be enlisted in the recovery process?

Creative Recovery

A recovery program is the systematic way that you deal with your addictive tendencies and your addiction problems. It requires a lot of you because it is predicated on the idea that an addiction is (or might become) a serious problem in your life, perhaps even a life-threatening problem. Your recovery program isn't something that you do after everything else or when you get the chance: you live it, you take it seriously, and you organize your life around your desire to live clean and sober (whether your problem is with alcohol or with some other substance or behavior).

The creative-recovery program presented here is the way you *honor* your creative nature by dealing with your addictive tendencies; the way you *serve* your creative nature by recovering from your addiction; the way you *use* your creative nature as part of the recovery process; the way you *create a life* that includes both creating and recovery; and the way you *educate yourself* about your risks for addiction, your patterns of addiction, and the details of your creative-recovery program. Throughout this book we will treat you as a creative person, as someone capable of imagining, feeling, reasoning, playing, daydreaming, concentrating, and everything else that a creative person can do.

We want to present you with a recovery program that takes into account your individuality, your creative aspirations, your oppositional edge, your drive, and the other personality qualities that make you the person you are. We intend to name the extra risk factors that challenge you by virtue of the fact that you are a creative individual and explain how that same individuality and creativity can be harnessed in the recovery process. We hope that you will feel met in our discussions and recognize these as your precise challenges and your best solutions.

Our Background

We come to this work in the following way. Eric is a licensed family therapist and a creativity coach and he has worked with creative people in these two capacities for more than twenty years. He has also counseled drinking drivers in the First Offender Program, a San Francisco–based, court-mandated diversion program. Susan is a licensed clinical psychologist, has maintained a private psychotherapy practice in Berkeley, California, for twenty years, and was a staff psychologist at the Stanford University Alcohol and Drug Treatment Center before joining the Chemical Dependency Services program at Kaiser Permanente. She's been active on panels at music-industry conferences such as South by Southwest, is on the editorial board of the journal *Medical Problems of Performing Artists*, and is the daughter of two professional musicians, bandleader Boyd Raeburn and jazz vocalist Ginnie Powell. Between us we've worked with lots of creative people and with lots of addicts—often enough, one and the same person.

We see recovery as the process of bravely acknowledging and mindfully dealing with an addiction. Most recovery programs are very helpful and provide important structure and sensible ideas. They demand that you deal with your defensiveness, change habits that have supported your addiction, make recovery a priority, and quickly return to the program when and if you lapse. Our goal is not to replace existing programs, as they tend to be strong and smart as they are. We only want to add something useful to them: a clear understanding of your special challenges as a creative person and sound advice about how to handle those specific challenges.

We are all would-be addicts, given the right circumstances of biology, psychology, and social setting. Some of us, because we are more at risk, become full-blown addicts and cross over into that place of obsession, compulsion, and loss of control known as addiction. Even if we don't succumb to an addiction, the odds are great that we feel a significant loss of control in some area of our life and have trouble maintaining a healthy weight, avoiding hours of Internet surfing, quieting our anxious thoughts, or staying on track with our goals. In order to deal with challenges of this sort, you need to recover: that is, you need to embrace a way of being that acknowledges and forthrightly addresses your addictive nature and your incipient problems.

If you don't, you might wake up one morning bound head to foot with a sturdy rope and murmur, "How interesting! I think I'll become a circus attraction!" Others have been down that road and are prepared to warn you against accepting that easy, happy bondage. Charlie Parker said, "Any musician who says he is playing better on tea, the needle, or when he is juiced is a plain straight liar." The poet John Berryman lamented, "Quart of whiskey a day for months working hard on a long poem. Wife hiding bottles, myself hiding bottles. Murderous and suicidal. Many hospitalizations, many alibis." The musician David Crosby admitted, "While I was an addict, I didn't write anything. I didn't have the attention span or the will." The happy bondage of an addiction is anything but happy— and not the answer. We want to teach you how to deal with the ties of addiction and live a creative, meaningful, addiction-free life that is characterized by freedom and not bondage.

SUSAN'S STORY

Like many professionals in the addictions field, I became interested in the work as a direct result of being affected significantly by addiction in my life. As a child growing up in Manhattan in the 1950s, I witnessed my parents drink, fight, and carouse as a backdrop to the more normal activities of our lives. My father, Boyd Raeburn, had an avant-garde jazz orchestra, which had been critically acclaimed as ahead of its time in the late 1940s but remained commercially unsuccessful. My mother, Ginnie Powell, was the vocalist for the band, having previously toured with Harry James and Gene Krupa. By the time my brother and I had arrived on the scene, the reign of the big bands was over, taking with it a noticeable piece of my parents' identities and musical careers. If the musician lifestyle had fueled parts of my parents' drinking before, financial stress and demoralization kept it going.

The subsequent relocation of our family to Nassau in the Bahamas, an alcohol-friendly resort environment, did nothing to slow down my parents' drinking. It just added paper drink umbrellas and suntan lotion. As fate would have it, my mother contracted meningitis in Nassau and died suddenly at the age of thirty-three. I was eight at the time; my brother was ten. Given that my father's response to his wife's untimely death was to keep drinking and go to live on a friend's sailboat, while my brother and I went to live with the alcoholic parents of a friend, one could say that we also lost all semblance of a normal father or home life as well. By the time I was twelve years old, my father had shipped us off to Los Angeles to live with nonalcoholic relatives. He died a few years later at the age of fifty-two, ostensibly from medical complications of a car accident. I always blamed the package of drinking, demoralization, and depression.

Although I had plenty of experience in the company of drunken adults who were sometimes charming but more often frightening or embarrassing in their behavior, I had little understanding of the addictive process or the long-lasting impact that living with and around alcoholics would have on me. I had heard about alcoholism but did not understand that I had been living with alcoholics. Despite—or perhaps because of—my emotionally complicated experience of parental alcoholism, I learned early on to consider drinking a natural, sophisticated, and generally desirable aspect of adult life.

As a young teenager, experimenting with alcohol seemed quite normal, given my family history and my precociously hip social environment. For the most part, drug use remained a foreign idea and something undesirable, something associated with scary people or with certain interesting individuals, like bebop musicians, who had ruined their lives for mysterious reasons. No one I knew did drugs or, if they were using, told me about it. Alcohol abuse remained the world I knew.

By the time I was seventeen, in the late 1960s in Los Angeles, the Summer of Love was in full swing; several of my coolest friends had started experimenting with drugs like marijuana, hallucinogens, and diet pills; and the process of my initiation into drug use began. This was my entry into the experimentation level on the abuse continuum. What might otherwise have remained a foreign concept—drug use—became a romantic and compelling reality. My era, social environment, and personal-risk profile came together in those heady days, producing a person familiar with alcohol and drugs and moving at a steady pace along the abuse continuum.

Slowly, through personal experience and by watching my friends, I learned about that continuum: levels of use that moved a person from abstinence to experimentation, social use, habitual use, abuse, and dependence. Fortunately for me, and despite a genetic vulnerability to addiction, I hovered in the habitual use of pot and alcohol for a couple of decades; experimented with cigarettes, speed, psychedelics, and pills; visited abuse but never lingered too long; and got off the elevator of addiction before it reached the basement floors of abuse and dependence. Many of my friends, relatives, and, later, my clients were not so lucky.

At about this time I was in graduate school, going to see a lot of bands. Along with others of my generation, I had already lived through the many headlines of musicians who mattered to us dying prematurely from their addictions. Somehow the death that really got to me was that of the singer Tim Buckley, who died of an alcohol and heroin overdose at the age of twenty-eight in 1975. I decided then to work with musicians as a psychologist and wrote a dissertation about musicians and their culture.

In 1985 my first cousin, Kim, dropped dead of heart failure related to his decade-long cocaine habit. He was as close to me as a second brother, as we were the same age and grew up together. I saw him drifting out to sea for years, and as hard as I tried to reach him and pull him back to the safe shore, I could not. But I did go to work at the Stanford University Alcohol and Drug Treatment Center soon thereafter to learn what I could about addiction and recovery.

Over the next ten years, two more of my longtime friends died in their thirties from their addictions. They both spun through cycles of recovery and relapse for years and finally lost their battles. Neither ever maintained an ongoing program of recovery. One relapsed on heroin and suffocated from respiratory failure alone in his van. The other fell seventy-five feet off a freeway overpass while driving drunk on his motorcycle and died in a U-Haul parking lot.

I sometimes glimpse my lost friends' faces, along with my cousin's, in the faces of my addicted clients and feel a wave of anger followed by a tsunami of sadness. I deal with this by rooting even harder for my clients, staying hopeful when they cannot. I can do this because I have also seen other friends, loved ones, and clients fully embrace recovery and stay clean and sober for decades. Watching them recover and grow over the years has been my truest education and most profound inspiration.

ERIC'S STORY

Like you, I have a creative nature and an addictive nature. I hope that I've demonstrated the former in my books. You have only to glimpse my insatiability at a buffet table to see the latter. Indeed, I could tell some eye-opening stories about that insatiability. But the story that I want to tell at this juncture isn't about using—it's about stopping.

One of the first things that happened after I enlisted in the army at the age of eighteen was that I started smoking. In the space of a few days I went from menthols to Marlboros to unfiltered Camels. Just that fast cigarettes owned me, in the way that anything possessing nicotine can own a body. I smoked in forbidden places, including around ammunition, I waited like a caged animal for smoke breaks, and I inhaled—the way every addict inhales his or her drug—ecstatically.

I was hooked at the level of biology and chemistry. I was also hooked at the level of metaphor and mythology. I identified with the Bogart of *Casablanca,* the world-weary, alienated, cynical loner who can't find any side to take except his own. Has nature fabricated any creature more susceptible to that particular myth than an urban eighteen-year-old fledgling writer who despises the war in Vietnam that his country is fighting? I was hooked on my Camels with different and equally powerful hooks: the one that chemically quelled my anxiety and the one that made me feel heroic, superior, and manly.

At the same time, I began reading Dostoevsky, Camus, Kafka—the existential classics—a reading regimen that cried out for those Camels (or, while in Paris, Gauloises, the cigarette favored by resistance fighters and by Picasso, Sartre, and Orwell and featured in the movies of Polanski and the spy novels of Le Carré). I read about authenticity and smoked anyway. I read about personal responsibility and smoked anyway. I read about freedom and smoked anyway. I smoked through walking pneumonia; I smoked in theaters, indifferent to the complaints of moviegoers; I smoked in restaurants, indifferent to the complaints of patrons. No one could tell me a thing.

Did my addiction render me immoral? Not quite, but it inclined me in that direction. I was more inclined (or compelled) to trample on the rights of others. I took every No Smoking sign as a personal affront and a call to action. I was more inclined to fib. Once you find the way to justify smoking to yourself, what else won't you find yourself able to justify? An active addiction helps take out your moral legs. I understood in a corner of consciousness that a truth-telling writer, the person I fancied I was or would become, could not really tell the truth while lying to himself that smoking was a reasonable activity, but I smoked anyway.

I was dependent on cigarettes. But that didn't mean that I had no independent thoughts, independent of the addiction. When I went on a river-rafting trip and found myself compelled to smoke in the middle of gorgeous nature, with river spray putting out my matches, I could see myself through my companions' eyes—and I saw an addict. When I scrambled around the apartment searching behind sofa cushions and in the backs of drawers for a cigarette, I knew what was going on. But I could muster no particular interest in stopping.

We'll discuss stages of change, the abuse continuum, risk factors—but what actually causes a person to decide to change? Is it always some "bottom," whether high or low, or is sometimes an accumulation of lessons, insights, experiences, and jolts that, with one last jolt, leads to a tipping-point moment? Can It ever be something as imprecise to define but as real as a growing maturity or a budding wisdom? In my case there was no terrible bottom: no medical emergency, no financial peril, no relational disaster. My young son made faces when I smoked: that mattered. My wife didn't smoke and knew better than to smoke: that mattered. One day, for no reason that I can name, I was able to picture a life without cigarettes: that mattered. I tipped over.

After fourteen years of smoking, something shifted. I decided that I wanted to live. But that isn't quite the same thing as deciding to quit. Rather than quitting, I determined to keep a record of each cigarette that I smoked, presuming that the cumulative effect of that record keeping would, at the very least, amount to a heightened awareness of the exact nature of my addiction. The main point was that a little record keeping was not going to interfere with my smoking—as I was not yet ready to quit.

I had an odd nonjob at that time, a job with no duties and no pay but that came with business cards. I used those business cards to record my cigarette intake, a new card each day, marking off cigarettes in that four-vertical-strokes–one-horizontal-stroke way, an identical forty-seven cigarettes every day. I smoked the same number at home in San Francisco, in Paris, in Budapest, in Seville, wherever I found myself: always two packs plus seven. That I smoked exactly the same number of cigarettes every day defies logic, but maybe addiction has its own logic and its own numbers.

Then, as my thirty-second birthday approached, I decided that I would actually quit. All of this odd preparation paid its dividends, and I felt calm and ready. On the day before my birthday I smoked my customary forty-seven cigarettes, recording each one with a stroke. On my birthday, after fourteen years of smoking, I stopped cold turkey, without a pang or a qualm, and haven't had a cigarette in the three decades since. Nor have I been tempted to resume.

It is fair to wonder what it means to say that a person is hooked on something if he can give it up from one day to the next without any physical or psychological distress. What sort of hook was it that it could be unhooked so easily? I think that the answer—the real and appropriate answer—is that any hook, no matter how deeply it has lodged itself, can sometimes come out cleanly. You can't guarantee such an easy recovery, and you had better not skip recovering just because you find recovery daunting. But it may serve you to hold in mind the possibility that recovery—because of your preparations, because of some deep sea change of heart, or for some mysterious reason that you will never be able to identify—need not be hell. Isn't that worth considering?

Creative Exercises

In order to maximize your active involvement with the information offered in each chapter, we'll provide five exercises, meant to reach different aspects of your creative self: the writer, visual artist, actor, dancer, musician, scientist, and dreamer in you. We encourage you to experiment with any or all of these aspects of your creative nature as you move through the exercises and the chapters.

The theme of this chapter's creative-recovery exercises is *addiction as bondage, recovery as freedom.* Try to engage as fully as you can with any exercise that piques your interest. If you notice that you are fiercely resistant to doing any of the exercises, become curious about that as well. If you want to make up additional exercises of your own, go for it! Your various responses to this process offer yet another source of information in the service of self-discovery.

To get started, find a welcoming space for yourself, free of interruptions; read the exercises; and try out one or another of them, including exercises in a genre that might be a stretch for you. Allow yourself to experiment freely, leaving your inner critic at the door as best you can.

As you do the exercises, we suggest further that you cultivate an attitude of playful and nonjudgmental observation of your experience. Some areas to notice include bodily sensations, visual images, memories or associations, emotions and their level of intensity, thoughts, behavioral impulses, and any judgments you make about having these responses. In other words, what aspects of your self-experience and creative nature become engaged around each chapter's topic? For our current chapter theme, notice which aspect, bondage or freedom, feels most immediate or powerful for you before you get started.

After each exercise, stop and reflect. Pay attention to your responses to the scenarios you've written. You may want to make some notes in your creative-recovery journal about these responses.

1. For the writer in you

Write a story with a contemporary setting in which a person wakes up and finds himself or herself bound in some way—and takes no measures to get unbound. Describe the bondage. Is it more emotional, physical, situational, or existential or spiritual? Play out that absurd scenario in which your main character knows better but allows it to continue anyway.

Continue by writing an ending to the story in which your character stays bound indefinitely; what are the personal consequences for your character and/or the people around him or her? Then write a second ending in which your character makes a break toward freedom; how was he or she able to do that? How does the story develop after that?

2. For the visual artist in you

Depict your addictive bonds, whatever they may be. What materials does the expression of these bonds seem to require: paper and collage, oil paint, watercolors, charcoal, clay, wood, plastic, steel? How does it feel to engage in this piece?

Now do a companion piece on the theme of freedom from bondage. What materials and colors are required for this piece? What does it feel like to work on this piece? Which piece was easier or most difficult to make? Which piece left you wanting to keep making art, as opposed to giving up or escaping?

3. For the actor in you

Imagine that you are given the role of playing a person who is starting to succumb to an addiction—but is not yet showing obvious signs of that addiction. How would you play that person? What cues or clues would you provide to communicate his risk? Now develop a scene in which that character begins to experience some discomfort associated with his addictive behavior. What would you want to show the audience about this character's development—past, present, and future?

Consider your responses to the scenes you've produced. Which aspects of the acting were the most compelling for you? Which were the easiest or the most difficult? What have you discovered about your responses as an actor to these themes of bondage and freedom?

4. For the scientist in you

Solve the following problem: a component of a system (addiction) is draining power from the rest of the system (the self), and no one but you can see the problem. How do you correct the problem without shutting down the larger system?

What does solving this problem teach you about bondage and freedom? Can you identify any parallel dilemmas in your own life? How does this apply to the expression of your creative nature?

5. For the dreamer in you

Imagine the most unfettered, freest you. What does that person look like and what does he or she do? What do you need to do to support that image of yourself? What actions interfere with it? Have you ever felt like that? When?

Postscript

When you have finished doing these exercises, take a moment to notice your overall responses to this theme of addiction as bondage, recovery as freedom. We remind you to listen in along the lines we suggested previously: bodily sensations, visual images, memories or associations, emotions and their level of intensity, thoughts, behavioral impulses, and any judgments you make about having these responses. Notice which aspect, bondage or freedom, feels most immediate or powerful for you *after* completing the exercises.

Identify which aspects of your self-experience and creative nature became engaged around this chapter's theme. Did doing the exercises have an impact on your relationship to the theme? Take that into consideration as you move into the next chapter.

PART ONE

Preparing

1 ◤ *Biological Risks*

What puts you at risk of an addiction? The answer is that it is more than any one thing. There is no single biological, psychological, social, environmental, spiritual, or existential factor that can account for anybody's addiction. These factors weave together, interact, magnify one another, and place one person at lesser risk and another person at greater risk. This chapter looks at the biological factors that can lead to addiction. And since you were born creative, this chapter also explores your inherent creative nature and how that may lead to greater risk for addiction.

Understanding What Risk Means

To say that someone is at a high risk for addiction doesn't mean that the person will become addicted. A high risk is not destiny. Nor, conversely, are seemingly low-risk individuals home free. Low-risk individuals can and do crash and burn into addiction as everyone around them wonders, "What happened?" You keep up your energy and spirits for twenty years as a midlist author; one day you look up and virtually all of your books are out of print, and your social drinking turns into binge drinking and looks headed for worse. Because triggers of this sort can and do produce devastating results, we must stand humbly before the reality that a person who looks to be at no particular risk for an addiction may be only one terrible review or one nasty rejection away from a fall.

Risk factors predispose you to an addiction. Then, once you start using, new risks arise. The substance you use or the behavior you engage in can affect your brain and begin to lock the addiction in place. For example, as a biological matter and a psychological matter, you may already have been inclined to take little interest in reality, social relationships, and the world around you. You were already at risk of becoming addicted to something that provided you with a fantasy life and kept reality at bay. Then you begin playing video games for hours, and your brain goes, "Wow, this is *exactly* what I've been looking for!" It starts to turn over its neuronal circuitry to an obsession with video games, making it that much harder for you to care about or deal with reality. You were primed to become hooked in exactly this way; then, when the right hook came along, it grabbed your brain and began to own it.

Once you voluntarily start using mind-altering substances or repeating mind-altering behaviors, your brain becomes modified in various predictable ways. If you continue to use repeatedly, your brain structure and function will be changed in long-lasting ways that can take on a life of their own even after you've stopped using. This is what researchers such as Alan Leshner, former director of the National Institute on Drug Abuse, mean when they claim that addiction is a brain disease. They mean that the brain, hooked on a certain fix and a certain feeling, begins to alter itself in the service of the addiction by changing its very structure. A dancer's hips are physically affected by the rigors of dancing; her brain is likewise physically affected by all the pain medication she takes.

Addiction develops through a series of brain changes that involve the strengthening of new memory connections in various circuits of the brain.

Negative changes in your ability to think clearly and to feel authentically eventually follow. Leshner explains, "It is as if drugs have hijacked your brain's natural motivational control circuits, resulting in drug use becoming the sole, or at least the top, motivational priority for the individual." People who carry a low genetic susceptibility may get out of the loop before this happens and may therefore have more room to experiment with addictive substances and behaviors. Conversely, someone who is at significant genetic or emotional risk may find his or her brain adapting quickly in service of the addiction.

What began as an easy pull toward pleasure, reward, or euphoria turns into a vicious cycle of cravings, compulsion, seeking, and using, with diminishing rewards and increasingly bad outcomes. Over time, addicts continue to chase that original high that never comes again. Known as euphoric recall, it is like continuing to go to a job that you once loved but no longer even like, one that is increasingly painful and where you've stopped getting a paycheck. In fact, now you have to pay the boss. You keep going, doing the same thing over and over again and expecting different results, a situation known in AA circles as the very definition of insanity.

Researchers Arnold Washton and Joan Zweben have said: "Chronic drug use brings with it a cycle of spiraling dysregulation of the brain's reward systems, eventually resulting in loss of control over drug taking and compulsive use. In time, this process changes the reward set-point in the brain, resulting in continuous relapse vulnerability that remains high even though the patient is abstinent." Once your brain gets addicted, you are typically no longer capable of maintaining psychological control over your use through willpower. That is why there is no simple addiction cure, only recovery through abstinence and cognitive, emotional, behavioral, and existential or spiritual self-regulation strategies.

When you think about risk, you should think about it in these two different senses: as predisposition and as brain change. In the first case, you are at risk of becoming addicted; in the second case, you are at risk of staying addicted by virtue of the fact that your brain has changed its neural chemistry to support the addiction. Imagine being predisposed to clutching an egg in your hand. Not only are you at risk of finding yourself always holding an egg, but you are also at risk, once you start clutching eggs, of your hand's shaping itself into a rigid claw. Even when an egg isn't there, your hand is still claw shaped—not the best shape for holding your paintbrush or typing away at your novel! But before you begin to feel too defeated, remember that there are viable ways to change your brain in support of healthy behaviors. We'll explore both the biological risks you may encounter and ways your brain can heal from addictive habits.

CREATIVE-RECOVERY JOURNAL QUESTIONS

1. Do you have any sense of what addictions you might be prewired for? Have you had intimations or inklings that you are seriously vulnerable to the grip of some particular substance or behavior?
2. What would happen to your brain if it found its perfect fix? How quickly and completely do you think it would reconfigure itself in the service of repeating that experience?
3. When you repeatedly do something that produces only negative outcomes, how do you explain that situation to yourself? What is your typical rationale for continuing something that you know is harming you?

Biological Risk Factors

Having a biological or genetic predisposition for addiction means that the biological material or genes that have been passed on from a set of parents to their child can increase the probability that the child will develop an addiction, if and when the child is exposed to particular mind-altering substances or behaviors. In exactly the same way, people inherit genetic predispositions for other sorts of problems such as cancer or heart disease. As Jane Brody put it in the *New York Times:* "A genetic predisposition is just that: it is not destiny, but rather a tendency that can be encouraged or discouraged to express itself by how we live our lives."

Sometimes this genetic risk is small and sometimes it is very large. Dr. Nora Volkow, director of the National Institute on Drug Abuse, has estimated that about 50 percent of a person's vulnerability to addiction is genetic. She says, "If you're never exposed to illegal drugs, or if you grow up and live in an environment without trauma and too many stressors, you probably won't get addicted." By this she means that if our genetic risk to a given addiction is "only" 50 percent of the picture, no one is absolutely sentenced to an addiction. It will take other factors, such as a difficult childhood or an anxious personality, to tip us over the edge. Nevertheless, if our biological susceptibility to addiction can indeed be as high as the 50 percent level, then it is most likely the single greatest risk factor for addiction. As a consequence, you should carefully evaluate your biological risk factors.

Of course, you can't measure your genetic risk or your genetic disposition directly or perfectly. You can do so only obliquely, using the following four markers: your family's history of addiction, your level of tolerance with respect to the initial effects of alcohol and drug use, your tendencies toward high anxiety and engaging in sensation-seeking behaviors, and the extent to which you are more of a stop or a go sort of person. If many of your family members are alcoholics, if you have a high tolerance for alcohol, if you have an anxious personality yet love to seek out novel or dangerous experiences, and if your tendency is to go for things rather than stop yourself, that picture translates as high biological risk for addiction.

Scientists base their understanding of genetic risk factors on a variety of research studies, including animal studies, family histories of people who are in formal treatment for addiction, brain-imaging techniques, twin studies, and adoption studies. Although alcoholism has been by far the most studied of the addictions, there is growing scientific support for what has been called the general genetic-risk hypothesis. This theory asserts that genetics can account for a general vulnerability to addiction across all mind-altering substances (alcohol, marijuana, cocaine, and so on) and across all mind-altering behaviors (gambling, binge eating, sexuality, shopping, Internet use, and so forth).

This means that if you are at biological or genetic risk for one addiction, you could be at risk for many or all of them. The Harvard addictions researcher Howard Shaffer concluded that each separate addiction disorder only represents a distinct expression of the same underlying addiction syndrome. Separate expressions of addiction can also interact and reinforce one another, forming addictive "packages" that are more than the sum of their parts. This means, to use the above example, that if many of your family members are alcoholics, if you have a high tolerance for alcohol, and if you have any of the four risk markers we described above, depending on your personality you may find yourself gravitating toward a sex addiction or an eating disorder rather than alcoholism or else toward a package of addictions that may or may not include alcoholism. Markers like a family history of addiction or high tolerance should alert you to the fact that you are primed to become addicted to *something*.

Along the same lines, Dr. Patrick Carnes, a researcher in the sexual addiction field, has described the tendencies of addicts to combine mood-altering chemicals with mood-altering behaviors and has floated the idea of an addiction interaction disorder with biological, psychological, and developmental components. Carnes explains: "Each addiction or deprivation/avoidance pattern has not only unique qualities but remarkably similar characteristics. Thus, the same patterns of loss of control or super efforts to control appear repeatedly driven by the same list of internal dynamics including shame, escapism, trauma, and stress."

Carnes has argued that addiction often involves extreme behaviors at either end of a control spectrum, with initial overcontrol linking to subsequent lack of control, and that distinctly different expressions of addiction can interact, reinforce, and merge with one another, forming addictive packages. Treatment then needs to be directed at these addictive packages rather than focusing on a prominent aspect of an addiction, such as chemical dependency. It is easy to imagine that there must be some underlying biological link that connects these behaviors and that produces these patterns, making one addiction look so much like another.

Of course, this is no exact science. But according to these studies, if one of your biological parents was alcoholic, you have a three- to four-times-higher risk of becoming alcoholic yourself once you start drinking than if you had no family history of addiction. Similarly, the greater the number of alcoholic relatives you have, the biologically closer the relatives are (for instance, your father rather than your second cousin), and the more severely the relatives were addicted (for example, your grandfather died of alcohol-related causes), the greater your risk of developing an addiction.

Your family history provides what looks like solid information about your biological risk factors. So does your level of tolerance, for alcohol or for any other substance or behavior that happens to threaten you. High tolerance is a significant danger sign and has a specific biological meaning. Dr. Marc Schuckit has found that in individuals who manifest the same blood-alcohol level, those with a family history of alcoholism have less intense subjective feelings of intoxication than do people with no such family history. That is, if I can get high on one beer but it takes you six beers to experience the same feeling—the feeling we are both after—then you will drink those six beers; over time, that will change your brain chemistry and have your body regularly demanding those six beers. You and I are after the same experience, but you have to drink alcoholically to get it.

People who can drink their friends under the table also tend not to experience the usual negative consequences of drunkenness, such as hangovers, that would teach them to slow down or stop their drinking. So not only do they have to drink more to get the same high, but at least initially they experience fewer physical consequences from the amount they drink. Their very ability to drink is a serious biological problem—and a significant red flag. If you have been taking pride in your ability to drink (or to take anything or do anything more than your peers), it is time to switch your mind and see that very ability as a red flag and not a blessing.

Two other, almost certainly related, biological risk factors are high anxiety and sensation-seeking behavior. Sons of alcoholics, for instance, demonstrate higher than normal levels of anxiety on a number of measures, and it has been theorized that drinking and using become a way for anxious people to self-medicate. This propensity often corresponds to higher levels of agitation, impulsive urges to act out, and thrill-seeking or sensation-seeking behaviors. Marvin Zuckerman and others have described sensation seeking as "the tendency to seek novel, varied, complex and intense sensations and experiences and the willingness to take risks for the sake of such experience." This twin package—high anxiety cou-pled with the inner plan to deal with that anxiety through dangerous tactics that mask or counteract the anxiety—looks to be a special and significant genetically based risk factor for addiction.

Another aspect of inherited vulnerability to addiction involves two critical brain systems, what the researcher A. R. Childress has described as the ancient Stop! and Go! circuitry of the brain. The stop system is respon-sible for inhibition, for managing our impulses toward reward, and for looking past immediate gratification to the consequences ahead—to put-ting the brakes on. Conversely, the go system underlies our pull toward natural rewards, such as food and sex, and helps us calibrate the degree of our response to drugs. As with other aspects of inherited vulnerability to addiction, people are not born equal in their brain's capacity to stop and to go. Some people are more stop; some people are more go.

Let's take a look at a case study from Susan's clinical practice to help us get a better handle on how these biological risk factors combine and interact with other factors to produce serious negative consequences.

The Case of Ken

Ken T. was a wood sculptor who became a cocaine addict and died from his disease at the age of forty. Both of his grandfathers and his maternal grandmother were alcoholics, and only the latter became sober during the time that Ken was growing up.

Ken demonstrated a high tolerance for alcohol once he started drink-ing, but he did not start drinking or smoking pot regularly until he was over eighteen. He'd experienced serious foot problems as a small boy that affected his mobility and left him feeling painfully self-conscious around other kids. While his peers were playing sports in the neighborhood, he preferred spending time alone and discovered that he was especially good at carving wood into animals and figures.

Ken grew up in a household with a loving but highly anxious and controlling mother who had experienced sexual abuse as a young girl in a foster family, where she was placed to remove her from her alcoholic mother. Although Ken's maternal grandmother eventually got sober, his mother displayed many characteristics associated with being an adult child of an alcoholic. As a former dancer, she took an active interest in her son's creative nature and encouraged his woodwork, buying him art supplies and books about wood sculpture.

When he was a young boy, Ken's father had found himself abandoned by his alcoholic dad. As a consequence, his own fathering skills were severely limited. In addition, he was a traveling salesman and absent for long periods of time. When he returned home, Ken's father was an immature, narcissistic, and rejecting parent and highly critical of his son. He would make fun of his son's artwork, calling it girlish, and Ken learned to keep his artistic activities out of sight when his dad was at home.

Open verbal conflicts between Ken's parents were typical occurrences during these periods. Ken's father was also regularly physically abusive to Ken. His mother talked openly about only staying in the marriage for the sake of the children and finally divorced his father when Ken was seventeen.

Ken began using marijuana and alcohol soon after his parents' divorce and maintained a habitual pattern until he was in his mid-twenties, with no obvious problems. In his late twenties Ken relocated to a new city after a breakup with a long-term girlfriend and started socializing with wealthier, musician friends who habitually used cocaine.

By this time Ken had become a carpenter to pay the rent, while sculpting in wood remained his avocation. He didn't have the financial resources to keep pace socially with his new acquaintances even though he desperately needed to feel accepted by them. He admired their creativity and envied the apparent freedom of their lives.

Ken's habitual use of pot and alcohol and occasional use of cocaine soon morphed into a serious cocaine habit. He became stagnant creatively, stopped sculpting altogether, and continued to use. He began dealing cocaine to maintain his habit and to secure his place in his social circle. This easy access to his drug of choice increased his use and accelerated his death.

Ken's biological risks for addiction were high by virtue of his family history and his tolerance for alcohol. His psychological risk factors were significant and included his early physical problems and resultant self-esteem issues, an insecure attachment with a chronically critical father, and adverse childhood experiences, including intermittent physical abuse and chronic parental conflict leading to divorce. These risk factors were later greatly compounded by his social environment and his increased access to cocaine. Ultimately, his creative nature was no match for the addictive power of his drug habit. Ken epitomized risk—and traveled in the fast lane to death.

Ken's biological risks did not and could not tell the whole story, but the warning signs were there, just as they may be there for you. Ken refused to engage in the kind of self-analysis that we're promoting, and so his high tolerance for alcohol, his family history of alcoholism, and his other apparent and abundant risk factors never captured his attention, even in the context of the limited psychotherapy that he engaged in with Susan. We hope that you will use your brain's willingness to entrain new neural circuits and entertain new learning to educate yourself about your risk for addiction—and if that risk appears high, to wake up *right now* to the dangers you face.

There are many baseline biological differences among people—including gender, race, intelligence, sexual orientation, and so on. Every significant difference that you can name between two people may, in a given case, turn out to be significant in terms of the one person's higher biological risk for addiction and the other person's lower risk. Nevertheless, the four risk factors that we just discussed are well established in the literature and are the ones to which you should pay the most attention (along with a fifth risk that we'll describe in a moment).

CREATIVE-RECOVERY JOURNAL QUESTIONS

Think about your problematic behaviors. For each behavior (your alcohol use, your cocaine use, your gambling, your overeating, and so on) answer the following questions. We'll frame the questions in terms of alcohol use; substitute your own problematic behavior.

1. Can you drink more than the average person? When you drink exactly as much as someone else, do you get less high? When you drink a lot, are you spared hangovers and other consequences that would alert you to the problematic nature of your drinking?
2. Do you feel that drinking is in your blood, that it is something for which you have a real ability and with which you have a real affinity?
3. Describe your understanding of the relationship between tolerance and addiction as it applies in your life. Imagine that you have a low or no tolerance for alcohol. How would that change your relationship to alcohol?

4. Are you more of a stop sort of person or more of a go sort of person?
5. Can you provide yourself with some concrete examples of how you stopped when others went on or, conversely, how you went on when others stopped? What do these examples imply about your particular braking system?

Creativity and Individuality as Risks

Next we'd like to present a fifth risk factor that has so far escaped research scrutiny: the risk associated with a felt sense of individuality.

Like most people, you probably associate creativity with ideas like talent, ability, imagination, and so on. While these perceptions are accurate, we would like you to shift your thinking and begin to associate creativity with the following idea: that it is an expression of individuality, an expression of a person's desire to manifest her potential, to speak in her own voice, to have her own opinions, and to do her own work.

Creativity isn't just a trait or a set of traits: it arises because a person feels the need to be herself: to know what she knows, to love what she loves, and to do what she needs to do. Children don't draw because they have fingers or sing because they have vocal chords. They draw because they have a giraffe inside that needs to get out and they sing because they are bursting with song.

What distinguishes the creative person from other people is the creative person's felt sense of individuality. Many people are born conventional and find it quite easy to follow the crowd; only some people are born with a strong desire to assert their individuality. All the personality traits that creative people manifest—the more than seventy-five traits that have been described in the creativity literature—flow from this single core quality: the need to assert individuality.

Plenty of research has been conducted on the differences between highly intelligent adolescents and highly creative adolescents. All the research confirms a basic point: the creative person is not more intelligent than her peers or more gifted than her peers, but she is more individual than her peers. For example, John Holland found that creative high school students were "independent, intellectually expressive, asocial, consciously original, and had high aspirations for future achievement." Emanuel Hammer argued that highly creative art students placed an emphasis on "self-directedness, independence, criticality, and individuality," and Norma Trowbridge concluded that creative adolescents conform less and exhibit more self-motivation.

This individuality is a genetic orientation. A person is born individual or conventional—and within just a few years of birth she will feel that difference as she looks around her and finds herself unable to understand why the conventional people around her are acting so conventionally. As a result she is likely to start to feel alienated, out of place, like a stranger in a strange land. Even if she trains herself to hold her tongue and engage in conventional work, an individual of this sort will already know as a young child that she can't really conform and that she wasn't built to conform. To call this budding creator a nonconformist is only to call her an individual. They are different ways of saying the same thing.

Such an individual feels her individuality in her bones and begins to recognize that creating, which is already starting to interest her as she falls in love with books, music, or the constellations, is going to put her at odds with the conventional people around her. Her goal is to be individual, not oppositional, but because she must continually battle her conventional peers for her right to be individual, she becomes oppositional. A certain oppositional attitude naturally and inevitably flows from an individual's adamant effort to make personal sense of the world.

Arnold Ludwig, in his study of a thousand well-known creators throughout history entitled *The Price of Greatness,* had this to say about his subjects: "These individuals often have an attitude set that is oppositional in nature. It is almost as though this response set is part of their very nature. This antagonism to traditional beliefs, practices and established forms of authority assumes many forms. What distinguishes these individuals from others is that they do not simply rebel. These are not people who just see that the emperor has no clothes; they offer their own brand of attire for him to wear. They feel obliged to speak out, do what they believe is right, and pursue their own goals, even when they may be punished for doing so."

You probably sense that you came into the world as an individual, that this individuality is the source of your creativity and your need to experiment and try new things, and that you regularly feel thwarted and frustrated by the oh-so-conventional universe. Creative people move as fast as a ski jumper down a ramp toward reckless ways of dealing with the anxious feelings that this alienation and frustration produce. This is not an idle state: the creative person is not only an individual, she is driven to *be* that individual, a drive that sets her off racing through life.

This drive can be a risk in and of itself. Nature makes the calculation that for an individual to truly be individual, it had better invest her with enough power, passion, energy, and appetite to manifest that individuality. Otherwise individuality would be a cosmic joke, and nature doesn't joke that way. So it invests this individual with extra drive. Just as it makes no sense to produce a creature that enjoys the leaves at the tops of trees without also providing it with a long neck, so it makes no sense to produce a creature who is built to assert her individuality without providing her with the energy of assertion. This nature does.

As a result many creative people have more energy, bigger appetites, stronger needs, greater passion, more aliveness, bigger "ups," more adrenaline, more sex hormones, and more avidity than the next person. It is nature's way of fueling the individual so that he or she can *be* individual. It should also be clear how this extra energy and greater appetite often lead to conditions such as addiction, mania, and insatiability. How can you have an outsize sex drive and not become obsessed with sex? How can you have a ton of energy and not court mania? How can you have extra adrenaline shoot through your system and not need to race a hundred miles an hour down the road or gulp more than several drinks to take the edge off? Nature, by fitting some individuals with enough energy to write symphonies and to penetrate the mysteries of the universe, inadvertently creates a driven, insatiable, addiction-prone creature.

One of the major unfortunate consequences of this extra drive—this extra ambition, egotism, energy, passion, and appetite—with which nature imbues some individuals is that these particular individuals are hard-pressed, and often completely unable, to feel satisfied. A pressured creator eats a hundred peanuts—not satisfying enough. He writes a good book—not satisfying enough. He has a shot of scotch—not satisfying enough. He wins the Nobel Prize—not satisfying enough. This inability to get satisfied produces a background unhappiness and tension—a core anxiety—in this creative person's life and makes him want some experience that will mask this feeling or make it go away. So he has another hundred peanuts, so as to provide himself with some relief—without, however, coming any closer to actually satisfying himself.

It is as if nature turbocharged some of its creatures and then failed to give them a decent braking system. It provided extra energy, and with it a susceptibility to mania. It provided extra ambition, and with it a susceptibility to grandiosity. It provided extra appetite, and with it a susceptibility to promiscuity, obesity (or stubborn anorexia), and alcoholism. It provided extra adrenaline, and with it a susceptibility to car wrecks. If all of these extras could be channeled and regulated, we might thank nature for its largesse. As it is, these extras can make the creative person's life wild and unruly.

So nature creates an individual who must know for himself, follow his own path, and be himself; puts it in his mind that he is born to do special work; gives him the energy to pursue this work and the courage to stand in opposition to those who would prevent him from walking his idiosyncratic path; and then turns around and tortures him by doing nothing to relieve his core anxiety. Instead, it heightens that anxiety by giving him an existential outlook or a spiritual thirst, making sure that nothing will ever satisfy him, pouring adrenaline through his system, and swelling his head just enough that he tips over, top-heavy, into self-centeredness. All of this makes the work of creating that much harder and life a series of frustrating struggles. To repeat, not every creative person resembles this picture—but many do.

For people who are creative *and* who are harmed, deflected, or thwarted in such a way that their individuality and creativity are prevented from manifesting themselves, the risk for addiction is equally high. These many thwarted creative individuals, tens of millions of them, know exactly how soulful, satisfying, and special it would be to write a novel, engage in fascinating research, or invent new technologies. But they are prevented from doing creative work and standing up for their individuality by the harm done to them (we'll discuss this further in the next chapter, which addresses developmental risks). These are the world's world-be artists or, as the psychoanalyst Otto Rank famously dubbed them, the world's artist manqués. Their risk for addiction is heightened because of this core frustration, that they have been prevented from manifesting their potential. The working artist drinks because he is driven, the would-be artist drinks to drown his frustrations—and the typical creative person, who is sometimes effective and sometimes blocked, finds himself confronted by both reasons to drink.

It turns out that most creative people are a mixture of these two types, active, effective, driven, and creative in one area of their life or during one time period and passive, ineffective, unmotivated, and thwarted in another area of their life or during another time period. A poet may have a fertile two years and then a stagnant five years. A researcher may delve deeply into a subject that interests her and then find no similarly engrossing subject for the next decade. The reality is that most creative people will experience both sets of challenges: the challenges that come as they try to manifest their individuality and the challenges that come from failing to express their individuality—and the extra risk for addiction that both sets of challenges bring.

Individuality adds to your risk for addiction—and so does suppressed individuality. The drive to manifest your potential adds to your risk for addiction—and so does tamping that drive down. Growing oppositional adds to your risk for addiction—and remaining too obedient and doing violence to your nature also adds to your risk for addiction. We are betting that this makes perfect sense to you and that it matches your felt sense of reality and the complexities that you know exist. Who wouldn't break free of an addiction if addiction were a simpler matter than this? But it is exactly this knotty.

The greater the extent to which individuality (and thwarted individuality) has flowed through your family—the more novelists, frustrated musicians, inventors, frustrated explorers, iconoclasts, and so on that you can number in your family history—the more likely it is that you carry the individuality marker, and that makes you more at risk for addiction. Naturally this is an impressionistic and intuitive matter, trying to decide whether a given family member looks to be more individual or more conventional. Yet we draw those conclusions all the time, recognizing in Aunt Rose some spark or quality that we simply don't see in Uncle Max. If you give it some thought, you will no doubt be able to do this intuiting and decide for yourself to what extent you come more from a family of individuals (or frustrated individuals) or from a family of conventionals, and if the former looks to be the case, to what extent that adds to your risk for addiction.

CREATIVE-RECOVERY JOURNAL QUESTIONS

Consider how the fifth risk, of individuality, may affect your vulnerability to an addiction.

1. Do you sense a connection in your own being between being born individual and being at risk for an addiction?
2. What sort of added risk would it be to be born individual and then to have your ability to manifest that individuality thwarted and frustrated, say because your conservative parents felt chronically overwhelmed by your nonconforming nature, because as an adult the marketplace isn't interested in your fiction, because you chose a "safe" profession as a graphic artist rather than the risky profession of painter, and so on?

CREATIVE-RECOVERY EXERCISE

Draw your family tree, going as far back as you can, and identify the addictive patterns of each family member: the alcohol abuser, the overeater, the gambler, the sex addict, and so on. Be as creative as you like: make a photo collage, draw or paint an abstract or realistic tree, type the story of your family tree. Explore the addictive patterns of your family while also accessing your creative nature.

Try to do a nuanced job: that is, try to distinguish in your own mind whether Aunt Martha, who drank, was more a social drinker or more an alcohol abuser; whether Cousin Jack, who loved the horses, was more a recreational gambler or was really hooked on betting; and so on. If you can, attempt the next degree of subtlety by making note of your teetotaler uncle who didn't drink because he knew that he would drink abusively if he started drinking, and all the other nuanced quirks and behaviors that real people exhibit.

Next, try to identify which members of your family look to have been individuals (or thwarted individuals) and which ones look to have been more conventional. Has Cousin Larry always wanted to start a band, even though he ended up an accountant? Was your great-grandfather on your mother's side a cowboy poet? To continue this investigation, see if there is a strong correlation between individuality (or thwarted individuality) and addiction in these family members.

This exercise won't help you arrive at some perfect mathematical understanding of your biological risk factors. But we think that you will find it eye-opening and illuminating. If you discover that there have been many addicted individuals and many addicted thwarted individuals in your family history, it may begin to dawn on you that something really is going on at the level of biology and genetics throughout your family and also in your own system. It may wake you up to the fact that your heredity really does put you at risk. Once you understand that, it should make you more open to appreciating the threats that you face from deep within.

Old-Brain Threats and New Learning

One important aspect of your genetic or biological risk for addiction is the very way the human brain has evolved. Your brain can engage in very advanced activities like writing novels, composing symphonies, or deducing mathematical theorems. But side-by-side with that thoughtful, high-functioning brain is an ancient brain that is susceptible to the blandishments of pleasure. It wants what it wants, even when what it wants is not really in the best interests of the organism.

In the service of survival adaptation over millions of years, the human brain has evolved in three stages into two major parts, the old, or primitive, brain and the new brain, or neocortex. Whereas the brain of a rat has the majority of its functions dedicated to basic survival needs, more than half of the neocortex in the human brain is open for developing new synapses, new networks, and new learning. The new brain gives us the capacity to use numbers and language, to develop memory, to reason and figure out problems, and to perform other higher-order functions such as seeking novelty, using divergent thinking, and creating.

The reward center, colloquially known as the hedonic highway, is a powerful old-brain influence that keeps us vulnerable to the lure of pleasure fixes. It is also the area most affected by psychoactive substances. People with defects in this brain region are thought to be less satisfied by natural rewards, such as they might get from a good meal or a stroll through nature, and more prone to look for acquired highs from substances or from intense thrill-seeking behaviors.

Of course, you can't poke inside your brain and look for defects. Nor would you have any idea what manipulations to perform even if you could poke around in there. But it is important to remember that your brain is constructed this way, with old-brain pressures operating side by side with new-brain capabilities, and that some significant portion of your vulnerability to addiction may be structural and biochemical in nature.

If you are burdened by the risk factors we've discussed in this chapter—a family history of addiction, a family history of individuality and creativity, high tolerance, and so on—it should make extremely good sense to you not to add addictive substances or addictive behaviors to the mix. Most people are relatively successful at integrating the physiological drives of the old brain with the higher-order functions of the new brain—but because of your biology, you may not be "most people."

Psychoactive substances can derail this integration of old and new brain functioning by taking over basic survival mechanisms. By producing brief, intense stimulation, they can prove more powerful than natural rewards of longer duration and less intense stimulation. Even when the resulting addictive practices are clearly self-destructive, the pull of the reward/pleasure center of the old brain can be stronger than the moderating influences of the new brain. The more frequently the addictive substance is used or the behavior is repeated, the greater the brain change and the more difficult it is to restore normalcy. Why head down this path and play into the hands of your old brain and the lure of your reward center?

We hope that this brief discussion helps you better understand something that is otherwise difficult to fathom. How can a sensible, responsible, moral, creative person who loves life and wants to realize her dreams, accomplish her goals, and make meaning get hooked on a drug or a behavior to the extent that her addiction takes over and ruins her life? How can a beautiful, thin-at-heart woman end up with an extra hundred pounds? Biology, and especially our ancient wiring, must be a crucial part of this story. If you choose to think of yourself as only rational and in control, you are leaving your lizard brain and your leopard brain out of the equation. They are there, and they matter profoundly, as secret arbiters of pleasure and reward.

CREATIVE-RECOVERY JOURNAL QUESTIONS

1. What do you take to be the implications of the sheer biological power of your reward center and its pull to pleasure on your risk for addiction and on the challenges of recovery?
2. Do you have the sense that there is a hungry leopard inside you who can't get satisfied? How well have you been able to control that leopard's agitated demands?
3. Does one of your addictions provide one sort of reward (say, distracting you from your experience of anxiety) while another addiction provides a different sort of reward (maybe providing you with a keen, immediate sense of pleasure)? Try to distinguish not only among your addictive behaviors but also among the differing rewards you are seeking by engaging in those behaviors.

CREATIVE-RECOVERY EXERCISE

Thoughtfully and patiently depict your dangerous behaviors and substances through written words, pictures, drawings, or song. Create a list that takes into account what you know to be true about yourself and your proclivities. Of these many dangerous pulls, which seem to be rooted more in biological predisposition than in psychology, development, or social circumstances?

For example, you may sense that your cigarette smoking is a function of the fact that everyone around you smoked when you were growing up and that if you weren't now dependent on the nicotine, you'd actually be able to quit. On the other hand, your overeating may seem to you rooted in some biological, perhaps metabolic, peculiarity, as evidenced by the fact that everyone in your family seems able to put on ten pounds in the blink of an eye.

In this example, your addiction to cigarettes isn't rooted in biological predisposition, although it is now held firmly in place because of the addictive power of nicotine. On the other hand, food really does seem to be your biological drug of choice. Engage in this analysis for yourself to determine where you are most at risk at the level of biological necessity.

The Good News of Brain Plasticity

What can you expect from the recovery process given your biological risk factors for addiction, your family history, your primitive brain needs, and all the rest? Before you become too discouraged by the biological risks we've put forth, know that recovery is possible. Your brain is not set in stone. Given what we understand about brain plasticity, you can expect a positive outcome from your recovery efforts, even if your biological risks are substantial.

We are born with an estimated twenty-three billion nerve cells and can expect one hundred trillion connections to develop among them. Over time, our interaction with the environment prunes the structure and chemistry of our brain, altering the way neural connections respond to external influences. Brain changes are particularly dramatic in the first ten years of life, which helps explain why so much developmental and psychological harm can occur in childhood. These pruning processes continue throughout life, but they operate at an increasingly slower rate, and the brain continues to develop its major connections only until about the early twenties. But the good news is that enough brain plasticity remains after adolescence that real changes and real recovery can occur at any time during your life span.

Recovery is possible only because of this lifelong capacity of your nervous system to modify its structure and its functions in response to new learning and new stimulation. This is known as brain plasticity, or neuroplasticity. Brain plasticity is a feature of normal brain development and also enables compensatory adaptation as the brain compensates for losses in function and maximizes remaining functions in the event of brain injury. A late novel builds on a lifetime of writing and living; likewise, recovery arises out of new understanding and new commitments. Both are possible because the brain does not turn to stone at some certain age.

The complex process of ongoing brain change and growth involves multiple levels of organization, modifications in existing neural circuits, and the development of new circuits. The neuroscientist Bryan Kolb explains: "When the nervous system changes, there is often a correlated change in behavior or psychological function. This behavioral change is known by names such as learning, memory, maturation, and recovery." Our brain is able to change, and as it does, so do we—in our behavior, in our wisdom, and even in the way we remember the past. This allows our next symphony to be even richer than our last, as we have grown and changed in the writing of our last one; and it allows for a sober tomorrow, even if yesterday we were drinking alcoholically.

As a general rule, the brain preserves those neural connections that are most frequently or most strongly activated. It follows that the process of recovery from addiction is most effective when it is assigned a high priority in your life, that is, when you engage in it often and with real energy. You may be powerless to eliminate an elevated genetic vulnerability to addiction, but you have the power to engage in the recovery process and to change your brain as you work your recovery program. You may be powerless to excise your primitive brain, but you can pursue recovery sooner rather than later and condition your brain to prefer recovery to addiction. These possibilities are available because your brain retains lifelong flexibility.

Recovery does not mean that you have pulled off some fine conjuring trick and that you can now use with impunity. Your brain's plasticity works both ways: it can adapt to healthy habits or it can adapt for addiction. Furthermore, there are limits to this brain plasticity, limits associated especially with childhood sexual abuse and psychological stress and trauma. If you already have only limited brain plasticity, you will want to make the most of that remaining promise by fully committing to your recovery program. You can keep writing as you age, but you may have to start taking naps or introduce new organizational schemes as your memory begins to fail; similarly, you can recover even if you have been an addict for years, but only if you make committed use of your remaining brain plasticity.

To repeat, there is no way that you can assess your biological risk for addiction with anything like precision. For one thing, you may have a thing for one drug and not for another, get easily caught up in one risky behavior and find another risky behavior completely boring, and stand in a different risk relationship to every single substance and behavior out there. No one can assess his or her risk perfectly. But as a creative person with a brain, an imagination, problem solving skills, and other important core qualities, you can do a better-than-average job of reflecting on your history and your proclivities and making educated guesses about your addictive tendencies.

You probably already have a good sense of what tempts your primitive brain and what doesn't seem to interest it very much, what your Uncle Jack's and your Aunt Ethel's drinking meant and how that relates to you, how your high anxiety drives you to certain behaviors, and so on. You know a lot about these matters already. The way to access what you know is to take the time and do the work of self-assessment.

Creative Exercises

To help you continue with your self-assessment process, we'll use this chapter's creative exercises in the service of identifying your biological risk of addiction. First, review what you've figured out so far about the addictive patterns in your early family and their impact on you. Explore where you are most at risk at the level of biological necessity by accessing your creative talents for doing the following five exercises. Be as serious, spontaneous, or silly as you like as you start out.

Notice if your approach, mood, or motivation changes as you do the exercises. Once again, pay attention to your bodily sensations, visual images, memories, associations, feelings and their intensity, thoughts, action impulses, any judgments you have about these responses, and anything else that comes up for you. Add these reflections to your creative-recovery journal after each exercise.

1. For the writer in you

Write a short story about the people in your family (including yourself), describing any addictive patterns that you observed, heard stories about, or suspected while growing up. Remember to include compulsive behaviors such as binge eating or gambling as well as substance abuse.

Describe the addicted characters in this story. Were their behaviors influenced by previous generations of the family? How? Describe what impact the addicted characters have had on your feelings, behaviors, and biological risks for addiction. Make note of your responses to the process of writing this story as well as to the content.

2. For the visual artist in you

Draw or paint your family tree in black-and-white, going as far back as you can, making it either abstract or realistic. Now choose a strong color that signifies your risks for addiction and add that color to your family tree wherever it belongs. See what emerges. Consider what this drawing or painting signifies about your personal risk for addiction based on family genetics. Note your various responses to the piece, the process, and your conclusions about your risk.

3. For the dancer in you

Create a series of movements depicting the feelings associated with carrying a powerful biological risk factor for addiction. Demonstrate the full range of emotion you experience as well as how these emotions affect your energy, motivation, and sense of balance. Now, create a corresponding series of movements depicting your responses to the possibility of overcoming those biological risks. What differences do you notice? When you have finished with both parts of the exercise, describe your responses.

4. For the scientist in you

Prepare three or four survey questions on biological risk factors for addiction for your first-degree relatives, which you may or may not ever ask them to answer. What would you want to know? How would you go about distinguishing a biological risk factor from other risks? From what you already know about your genetic background, what is your analysis of your own biological risk for addiction? Assess your emotional response and the practical implications.

5. For the dreamer in you

Imagine a world in which no one is at biological risk for an addiction. Describe how that world would be different from the real world in which you were raised or in which you currently reside. Take note of your responses when you have finished dreaming.

Postscript

When you have done as many of the exercises as you plan to do this time around, take a minute to reflect on what you have learned about your biological risk factors for addiction. As best you can tell with the information you have so far, does this risk factor apply to you? If so, is it a substantial factor or a minimal one?

What did you notice about using your creative nature in these exercises? Identify which aspects of your self-experience and creative nature became engaged around this chapter's theme. Did doing the exercises have an impact on your relationship to the theme? Take that into consideration as you move into the next chapter, where you will learn about additional risk factors for addiction.

2 ⫻ *Other Risks*

In this chapter we'll discuss addiction risks that arise from developmental and environmental factors. As we proceed through the chapter, please pause for some self-analysis. The information we're putting forth will help only if you reflect upon its relevance in your life.

To start, let's play a little game. First pick an important aspect of your personality: your meekness, say, or your anger, your anxiety, or something similar. Then ask yourself the following question, "Was I born anxious or have I learned to be anxious?" Answer the question using all the tools available to you as a creative person. Delve deeply into the mystery of your own personality but also have some fun with this!

Let's say that you answered the question, "Was I born anxious or was I made anxious?" with "Well, both." Next, try to apportion the exact percentage of each and explain your apportioning rationale. This might sound like, "I think I was 37 percent born anxious and 63 percent made anxious. I intuit that these are the right percentages because I sense a certain amount of unwavering anxiety in me that must come from just being a human being and another, larger amount, about double the first, that comes from growing up in a fire-and-brimstone, everyone-but-us-is-going-to-hell church and family."

Nice work—but don't stop there! Refine your conclusions some more. This might sound like, "Well, thinking about it, I believe that I was born 37 percent anxious; half of that comes from my basic human nature and half from my artist nature. I am basically anxious about dying, crashing in airplanes, and all of that, but I am equally anxious about getting these novels inside me written—and written well. Then, for the 63 percent where I was made anxious, I think about half of that comes from my development, from my particular parents, church, and culture, and the other half comes from the kinds of tasks and challenges that I set for myself, such as trying to write a really difficult novel and following that up with the more daunting task of writing an even harder novel."

You can see what this kind of reflection is about. It's a way to consider the different risk streams flowing in your system and gauge which is more like a rivulet and which is more like a rushing river. As you learned in the last chapter, biological factors only contribute to your overall risk for addiction. This exercise is meant to help you also take into account the developmental risk factors that we'll explore in this chapter. At the end of the chapter we'll ask you to try to name your particular risk factors for addiction and give each its individual weight, just as you did a moment ago, attributing different amounts to your biology, your family of origin, your adolescent experiences, your artistic nature, and so on.

Risk Factors Arising in Childhood

In this section we'd like to go over some of the basics about addiction risks that arise in childhood. You may not be able to judge (or remember) whether you formed a secure attachment with your mother and father in the first years of your life or gauge to what extent your needs were met in infancy, but we think it's important that you spend a little time considering the dynamics of childhood and how they may have influenced or significantly contributed to your current difficulties.

A parent's most basic job is to equip his or her child for adult life in several crucial areas. Three areas that initially develop in infancy and continue to develop in childhood are the capacity to form secure connections (also known as secure attachments) to others, the development of an authentic and coherent sense of oneself, and effective self-regulation of one's needs, emotions, thoughts, and behavioral impulses. In order to optimally equip their children with these necessary capacities, parents must be able to provide a safe, predictable, and emotionally responsive environment, especially in the first few years of life, when the child's developing brain organizes itself in direct relationship to the quality of his or her caregiver's attunement.

An infant requires his caregiver's gaze and emotional signals in order to regulate his own response to his inner and outer world. As the psychiatrist Tom Lewis and his colleagues explain, "If a parent can sense her child well—if she can tune into his wordless inner states and know what he feels—then he, too, will become skilled in reading the emotional world." The parent's presence, interest, care, and love are signs that he or she has attached to the child—signs that the child, even as a small infant, can read and that begin to affect her ability to attach to others. If the child is also an intelligent, sensitive, creative child, she will be even more attuned to the excellence—or inferiority—of that parental attachment.

Attachment refers to a child's internalized representations of emotional relationships based on repeated interactions with his or her caregivers. These early templates form the basic map for all later relationships. Developmental psychologists have identified three types of attachment patterns and their outcomes. The first is secure attachments. Here the caregiver is consistently attentive, responsive, and tender to the infant. This isn't just about the parent spending time with the infant but also that the parent is accurately responding to him emotionally.

The result of a secure attachment is that the child experiences his caregiver as a safe haven from which to explore the world and learns to trust that he can get his needs met through relationships with people. This pattern of secure attachment and emotional attunement develops the infant's ongoing capacity for effective self-regulation of arousal, emotion, and self-esteem; builds a foundation for adult resilience; and protects against addiction. For a creative child, this secure attachment allows her to safely do all the exploring that is in her heart to do and permits her to draw outside the lines, think outside the box, and accept and respect her own ideas.

Two forms of insecure attachment are insecure-avoidant attachment, where the caregiver is consistently cold, rejecting, and rigid toward the infant, and insecure-ambivalent attachment, where the caregiver is repeatedly distracted, unpredictable, and erratic toward the infant. Insecure attachments generally leave children more at risk of developing an addiction, as they have learned not to count on relationships and not to expect people to meet their deepest needs for connection or self-soothing. At some point substances and addictive behaviors providing an immediate relief from discomfort look to be the safer attachment bet. These insecure attachments also hinder a creative child's ability to identify as a creative person and explore the world around him and force him to look for activities that feel safer than creating. Ultimately he may become a frustrated creator who never manages to manifest his creative nature and who is at added risk for addiction because of his dissatisfaction with life.

Two other sets of powerful risk factors are adverse childhood experiences and childhood trauma. In a Kaiser Permanente–Centers for Disease Control and Prevention study of more than seventeen thousand middle-class American adults of diverse ethnicity in San Diego, California, Drs. R. F. Anda and V. J. Felitti found that the greater the number and intensity of negative childhood events reported, the greater the probability of adult addiction. They reported that traumatic childhood experiences were surprisingly common but also typically unrecognized or concealed and that the children involved rarely got the help they needed.

Ten categories of adverse childhood experiences were included in the study: parental addiction, parental separation or divorce, parental mental illness, parental battering, parental criminal behavior, psychological abuse of the child, physical abuse of the child, sexual abuse of the child, emotional neglect of the child, and physical neglect of the child. According to Anda and Felitti, 33 percent of the sample reported no adverse childhood experiences, and the remainder of the sample reported the following trauma "doses": 26 percent had one; 16 percent had two; 10 percent had three; and 16 percent had four or more. To extrapolate from these numbers, two-thirds of all children are likely to experience at least one negative childhood experience, and one in four is likely to experience three or more. If you have this legacy of pain and trauma to deal with, your risk for addiction is higher, as is the risk that you will become a thwarted or inconsistent creator.

Special risks to the creative person that arise in childhood are in addition to all of these. If you were thwarted in your ability to express yourself—if you were told to shut up, to blend in, to be a team player and not an individual, to bow down to authority, to censor yourself, and so on—that is likely to have curtailed your creativity, turned you into a would-be or thwarted artist, and presented you with the additional risk for addiction that frustration provides. Similarly, if you were told that a life in the arts would prove too hard; that only selfish, irresponsible people pursued their artistic inclinations; or that only crazy or weird people gravitated to the arts, those messages naturally inclined you to damp down your creativity, thwarting you over time—and increasing your chances for an addiction.

Most complicated of all is the interaction between a stubborn, gifted, creative child and her conventional, conservative environment, which produces, as we discussed in the last chapter, an oppositional child who wants to do things her own way, live her own life, and take her own risks. Thumbing her nose at convention, driven to learn for herself and to know for herself, and feeling some narcissistic grandiosity as she senses what she believes to be her superior qualities and abilities, she is likely to carelessly risk doing expressly those things that she has been told not to do. She thereby greatly increases her chances of addiction by introducing addictive substances and behaviors into her world at an early age. The child who sneaks a cigarette or a drink just to get her parents' goat may only be expressing her budding individuality—but she is also putting herself at added risk.

Your childhood risk factors flow from the quality of the parenting you experienced; the resulting quality of your relationships to others; your capacity to effectively manage your needs, thoughts, feelings, and impulses (that is, to self-regulate); your experience of childhood trauma; and the interaction between your creative nature and your childhood environment. Because your brain is most plastic during infancy and childhood, the patterns that get established during this period endure and are often exceedingly difficult to change as an adult. Since these effects are enduring, problems in these areas are strongly linked to vulnerability to addiction. As you assess your vulnerability to addiction, you must give these childhood factors their significant due. Let's do that now.

CREATIVE-RECOVERY JOURNAL QUESTIONS

1. Do you have the sense that you grew up with attentive parents who responded appropriately to your emotional needs? If you did, describe the good that did you, especially as inoculation against addiction. If you didn't, describe the harm that did you, especially as a risk factor for addiction.
2. Can you make a stab at calculating how the exact form of your insecure attachment, if that was your experience, has played itself out over time as an addiction risk factor or as addictive behavior?
3. Did you experience trauma, adverse childhood experiences, or stressful life events as a child? If you did, to what extent have these negative experiences increased your risk for addiction? Can you tell?
4. What experiences in your childhood hindered the development of your creative nature? In your estimation, to what extent has that hindrance proved a risk factor for addiction?
5. Did your creative nature cause you to experiment in risky or precocious ways in childhood? If it did, to what extent did that early experimentation contribute to your addictive problems?

CREATIVE-RECOVERY EXERCISES

1. Depict the story of your childhood, emphasizing its difficulties and disappointments. Next, tell the story of your childhood

emphasizing its strengths and pleasures. How do these stories differ? What do these differences signify about how selective memory works?

2. Think about these four specific words: loss, humiliation, help-lessness, and danger. Did you experience one or more of them to a significant degree in childhood? Creatively depict each emotion that you experienced through painting, drawing, song, story, or whatever medium suits you. As you work, evaluate the likelihood that this particular childhood experience has proven an influential risk factor for addiction in your life.

Risk Factors Arising in Adolescence

For the typical creative person, virtually no time is more disorienting, tumultuous, and alienating than adolescence, when the realization that you are an individual who is firmly embedded in a culture of convention becomes achingly apparent. School often holds little meaning for you, nor do the usual pursuits and activities of childhood, and at the same time you hardly feel secure in your budding artist's identity, so you are not yet ready to really break free. This inability to break free raises peer relationships and the rituals associated with them, such as parties, dances, and concerts, to a place of paramount importance. Already we see why a young artist might drink, take drugs, smoke cigarettes, binge and purge, and so on—all the reasons and warning signs are blazing there in bright neon.

With modern imaging techniques, neuroscientists have learned that adolescence is a time of complex brain growth and of potential vulnerability to the growing brain when and if it's exposed to addictive substances or behaviors. The teen brain undergoes an extensive restructuring in areas that affect language, reasoning, intuition, and the ability to resist impulses, plan, and delay gratification. The brain's frontal lobes are particularly important in these functions, serving as the brain's chief executive officer. When people begin using mind-altering substances or engage in addictive behaviors as teenagers, before their brains have finished developing, they significantly increase their risk of later addiction.

Anna Rose Childress, an addictions researcher from the University of Pennsylvania School of Medicine, states: "In normal adolescence, changes in the brain's 'Go!' system are powerfully evident, with hormonal changes readying the system's response to rewards (e.g., sexual opportunity) that will ensure the all-important attempt to reproduce. In contrast, the brain's 'Stop!' circuitry is not yet fully developed: the frontal lobes, so critical for good decision making, are now known to continue to mature well into the 20s. This asymmetry—a fully developed 'Go!' system and a vulnerable, not yet fully developed 'Stop!' system—may represent a critical period of vulnerability for exposure to powerfully rewarding drugs of abuse."

At the same time that an adolescent is standing open and vulnerable to the lure of go experiences, he is engaged in certain developmental tasks that, to the extent that he fails at them, put him at increased risk for addiction. The key developmental tasks of adolescence include establishing a sense of personal identity, including sexual identity; establishing a personal value system and developing a sense of the continuity of life experiences; resolving the parent-child relationship; leaving home, both physically and emotionally; establishing an individuated relationship with parents based on authentic identity, needs, and values; and resolving residual trauma and coming to terms with his personal limitations, vulnerabilities, early disappointments, or childhood abuse. This is a lot—and failure in even one of these areas produces a vulnerability to addiction.

A creative adolescent is further confronted by the developmental task of choosing a creative path, beginning to actually create, dealing with early criticism and rejection (of her performance in the school play, of her short story submission for the school literary magazine), measuring herself against the abilities of others (is she soloist material or only good enough to play at the back of the violin section?), and dealing with sharp pangs of envy (as someone else is featured in the dance recital or gets his sculpture prominently displayed at the head of the stairs). These are often painful and testing tasks, made harder by the fact that most of them are being encountered for the first time.

The developmental psychologist Ozzie Siegel described this period succinctly: "At most we can hope that by the end of adolescence there is a relatively solid foundation in these areas, that the person entering adulthood is more mature than the person who entered adolescence, that there is a relatively firm sense of purpose and direction, and that life choices derive from within and are based on a set of values and ideals which are experienced as belonging to the self." This may be the ideal, but many adolescents enter their first year of college or conservatory still completely up in the air and unsettled—and ripe for experiences that will soothe their nerves, like too many beers at the house of the local enabler.

Issues of personal identity, relationships to parents, and coming to terms with vulnerabilities and abuse are seldom fully resolved in adolescence. Individuals who grew up with secure attachments to their parents and without adverse childhood experiences are more likely to master the primary tasks of adolescence than those who did not. For most of us, the resolution of these issues continues to develop well into adulthood. For those who have suffered from adolescent mental health problems, who started using mind-altering substances or behaviors early on, or who lived with adverse childhood experiences such as chronic stress and trauma, the tasks of adolescent development can remain painfully frozen and unfinished, resulting in serious negative adult consequences and an increased risk of addiction.

The researcher Barbara Strauch explains: "While adolescence includes the more precise biological moment of puberty we most often associate with teenagers, it is not just a single moment but actually a series of stages, many of which are unseen, that begin long before the first breasts sprout, and last long after kids have left for college." The adolescent becomes more his or her own person—for better or for worse—and for many, certain difficulties in living begin to manifest themselves. Unanswerable chicken-and-egg questions begin to arise: is this depressed young adult drinking alcoholically because of his depression or is his alcoholic drinking causing his depression? For some, serious psychological issues or illnesses suddenly appear that are themselves impressive predictors of addiction.

Many studies have shown that people with emotional difficulties, and especially mental illness, are more likely to have problems with addiction— and vice versa, that if you're addicted, you're also likely to display some other clinical syndrome. As the medical researcher Kim Mueser and her colleagues state: "The lifetime prevalence of substance use disorders in persons with the more severe illnesses of schizophrenia and bipolar disorder is about 50%, compared to about 25–30% in persons with depression or anxiety disorders, and 10–15% for persons with no mental illness." Community samples of adolescents who are abusing substances have shown that about 60 percent of them also have diagnosable psychiatric conditions. What this means, simply put, is that adolescence is far more than a tumultuous time: for many, it's the time when their trademark biological and psychological vulnerabilities begin to manifest themselves.

Nor can we leave out the environment. Adolescence involves a series of dynamic interactions between your personality, which is both formed and also in flux, and your social and environmental milieu. Those precise social and environmental influences are themselves risk factors for addiction, above and beyond the risk factors embedded in your being. Some of these more "happen" to you, as, for instance, growing up in an alcohol-free culture, and others are personal choices, such as deciding to become an actor and thus inviting repeated criticism and rejection. But whether they are more an accident or a decision, they significantly affect your overall addictive picture.

Social and environmental risks are often divided into the categories of micro and macro. Micro influences include such things as the culture of your family, your friends, your immediate neighborhood, and your specific workplace. An example of a micro influence operating as an environmental risk factor is when a young musician plays in a bar and is expected to accept drinks from fans. Macro influences relate to the larger cultural environment, such as a person's community and country, with its institutions and especially its mass media. An example of a macro influence operating as an environmental risk factor is when a young writer buys into the cultural stereotype that creativity and addictive behavior are joined at the hip.

The adolescent is bombarded by these micro and macro influences. The creative adolescent who has decided to become a poet, say, is influenced by the way that poetry is respected by one small group of his peers and despised by the remaining, much larger, group; by the way that the culture plays up the drinking exploits of famous dead poets such as Dylan Thomas; by the way that writing poetry of alienation makes him feel that much more alienated; and by the way that the members of his own family, each in his or her own way, try to dissuade him from the poet's life.

Parents naturally continue to play a large role in all of this. Parental behaviors of support, nurturing, and monitoring, such as knowing where their kids are at night, and espousing values that demonstrate disapproval of potentially addictive behaviors, are environmental influences associated with lower levels of alcohol and drug use. Similarly, higher levels of parental involvement appear to moderate peer influences on drinking even for at-risk older adolescents. Other micro influences range from the way substance abuse is frowned upon, tolerated, or encouraged at school; the number of bars and liquor stores in your neighborhood; and the choices your friends make about how they recreate: are they more inclined to go hiking or to hide out behind the field and light up?

In evaluating how developmental and environmental factors interact, some studies suggest that social influences seem to be the most important factors in setting up initial use, but individual, developmental factors such as genetic predispositions, personality traits (such as a sensation-seeking nature), and untreated preexisting mental disorders appear to be better predictors of subsequent substance abuse and dependence. Who you are looks to be relatively more important than where you find yourself: a person inclined to sobriety will make for a sober actor, while a person inclined to addiction will make for a drunk accountant. This should remind you to focus, as you engage in your ongoing risk assessment, on the essentials of who you are: the essentials of your biology, your personality, and your creative nature.

CREATIVE-RECOVERY JOURNAL QUESTIONS

1. Did you start using early in adolescence, at a time when your

stop and go system was still forming? If so, can you calculate the consequences of that early use?

2. Did you have trouble (and are you still having trouble) establishing your own identity (including your sexual identity), resolving your relationship with your parents, and/or leaving home?
3. Have you worked through or are you still working through residual trauma issues from adolescence?
4. Did your overall experience of adolescence aim you in the right direction, away from addiction, or pull you in the wrong direction, toward addiction?
5. Do you suffer from a chronic case of the blues or anxiety that has dogged you since adolescence (or earlier) and that you've been inclined to medicate?

CREATIVE-RECOVERY EXERCISE

Rewrite or reimagine your adolescence (without changing your childhood) so that you now find yourself at reduced risk for addiction. How would that rewritten version of your adolescence read?

Creative-Nature Risk Factors

In chapter one we described your creative nature as a certain drive or inner pressure to be an individual and to realize your human potential, a drive that as likely as not puts you in opposition to conventional aspects of your family, community, and society at large. Both your personal inner drive and the environment in which that drive is manifested greatly affect your risk for addiction.

The Need to Make Meaning

One of the main aspects of being a creative person—and of striving for individuality—is that you feel responsible for making meaning in your life. Where this honorable stance leads is to regular meaning crises, since the activity you had invested meaning in—such as your singing career or your research career—will on some days be rendered less meaningful, or even meaningless, because, for example, no one is recording you or no one is funding you. Creators are prone to addictions because an addiction is an ineffective but tempting way to handle these recurrent meaning crises.

Why is your relationship to meaning such a risk factor? Say that you find little meaning in your day job. Your novel isn't going well, which is a second meaning drain. The hard work of creating is wearing you out, as is the hard work of filling up your seconds, minutes, and hours with meaning. You feel at odds with your culture and at odds with your world. A drink seems to help. Many drinks seem to help more. Drinking becomes an obsession; showing up at the neighborhood bar becomes a compulsion. Especially if you are burdened by some of the risk factors we've previously discussed, such as a biological propensity for addiction and early developmental traumas, you are staring an addiction straight in the face.

You begin to organize your life around your drinking, even though the drinking and its aftermath do not help your writing one bit, all romantic mythology about wild and crazy drunk authors notwithstanding. Indeed, you stop thinking about writing and you start thinking only about drinking. The ongoing meaning crisis and the void do not go away, but thinking about your next drink fills that void. The messes that you make; the self-recriminations, the scenes, the bargains you strike with yourself; all the dramas and tidying up, fill the void—only pathetically, to be sure, but no less successfully for that.

Now your friends talk more about getting you sober than about reading your new novel. You realize that you are on a downward slide and there is something a little heroic in your struggle to break the addiction—the heroism you might have lavished on your novel you lavish on fighting your addiction. The addiction takes the place of your creative efforts and becomes the thing that you think about, the thing that you crave, and the thing that you have dreams and nightmares about. It becomes your meaning—or rather, your meaning substitute. Does this sound familiar?

Without genuinely meaningful activities to pursue, your aliveness eventually turns to listlessness; you begin to be out of sorts and become ripe for distraction and addiction. Similarly, when you abandon your meaning-making efforts for whatever reason—because you find it too hard to make meaning, because you don't know what meaning to make, or because you've made some meaning and now want a respite from it—you court an addiction. Agitated, bored, you throw up your hands and cry, "Give me sex, give me a high, give me something—anything!"

Colin Wilson—the author of *The Occult, The Misfits,* and many other books—when chronicling the poet Lord Byron's love affairs with married women and young boys during the winter of 1818, explains: "Byron's chief problem was a simple one: he had no idea what to do with himself. He knew that he found social life boring and dissatisfying, but what was the alternative? Poetry might occupy a few hours of each day, but he spent the rest of his time wondering what he could do to keep himself amused. Life became an endless flight from boredom, rolling in his carriage all over Europe."

An addiction, although it reduces your freedom to make personal meaning and increases your psychological and physical dependence on the thing craved, nevertheless begins to take care of meaning crises in its own way, producing an oddly satisfactory state of affairs: the happy bondage we described in the introduction. The irony about addiction is that despite its terrible consequences, despite the guilt and despair that come from being out of control and knowing you are out of control, the addiction still seems less of a problem than do freedom and the challenges of making meaning.

The bondage is a real bondage but an almost happy bondage, for while addicted there is no question about how to fill your time. You drink and keep drinking, you sleep it off, you get sick, you go to the emergency room, you make scenes, you lose friends, you break bones. This, it turns out, is easier than sitting in the blinding sunlight and answering the question, "What healthy thing can I do with my freedom? In what meaningful project should I next invest my energy and my capital?"

The bound creator becomes devoted to his addiction and loses his ability to live authentically. He may become bound to anything: stock trading, *Star Trek* conventions, painting in a particular style. He may become bound to consuming peanuts by the pound, like Orson Welles, who ironically claimed to hate peanuts. She may become bound to planting flowers, like the poet and novelist May Sarton, who likened her gardening to an addiction. When you want to train your mind over *here*, where the real meaning is to be made, but your mind goes over *there*, to the happy place of peanuts, flowers, gin, or poker chips, you've become an addict.

Anxiety from Not Making Meaning

A person with vitality, passion, and energy—a person who is really alive—possesses roiling thoughts, big ideas, and insistent desires. These inevitably lead to obsessions and compulsions. When these obsessions and compulsions are channeled in a positive direction, so that, for example, a songwriter is only obsessed about the song on his mind and his only compulsion is to get that song down on paper, all is well. Then he is creative, engaged, productive, and alive.

But because a creator can only create for so many hours each day and because creating is anxiety-producing work that he may be inclined to avoid altogether, he is often left with undirected kilowatts of energy to redirect, as well as the need to relieve the anxiety of not creating. His large energy needing to be expended and his anxiety needing to be eased barrel him headlong toward some other outlet—and the possibility of addiction.

It is excellent if you obsess about your novel or your gene theory. It is wonderful if you feel compelled to write late into the night or if you feel driven to arrive at your lab in the wee hours of the morning. Your productive obsessions and compulsions are, in this case, nothing but the expression of your passionate meaning-making efforts. You should want to feel compelled to write your novel or your symphony, because if you do not feel compelled, that is the equivalent of taking insufficient interest in it. You don't want to obsess about your neighbor's untidy lawn, but you certainly do want to obsess about your own creative ideas.

May Sarton wrote in *At Seventy,* the journal of her seventieth year: "Perhaps the answer is not detachment, as I used to believe, but rather to be deeply involved in something, to be attached. I am attached in a thousand ways. The price of being attached 'in a thousand ways' is that there is never even twenty-four hours free of pressure, but this year I am clear in my mind that just this is what my life is all about, and what I have to learn (so late!) is to accept the multiple demands and understand that a rich life is bought at a high price in energy. If I can be wiser about not feeling so compulsive about everything, all will be well."

A person with this life energy at her disposal must cultivate the habit of productively obsessing, so that she works hard at her creative efforts. At the same time, she must prevent herself from sending her energy and her thoughts off in directions that harm her, toward slot machines, Internet sex chats, or the next bottle of vodka. And she must temporarily turn off even her productive obsessions so that, for example, she remembers that she has a child to pick up from school.

When something manages to reduce our core anxiety and provides a feeling of well-being, however fleetingly, we want to repeat that feeling. After a while, we can get hooked on that feeling and that anxiety relief. That something might be chocolate, a wager, an orgasm, a fix, a beer, or a comforting belief. We think about heaven, reduce or mask our experience of anxiety, and produce pleasure—or at least a respite from worry. We sip our cognac, reduce or mask our experience of anxiety, and feel better. We drive at a hundred miles an hour and, high on adrenaline and thrilled by the ride, produce pleasure and distance ourselves from our worries. Naturally we want that feeling again and again. Who wouldn't?

People want to reduce their experience of anxiety. The body is set up to help in this regard, turning potato chips into chemical pleasure and relaxation, turning an orgasm into chemical pleasure and relaxation, using the raucous hubbub of a bar to distract it from its worries. Every body knows these anxiety-reducing pleasures; some bodies become addicted to them. If you have big drives, big appetites, big challenges, and big anxieties, this dynamic is magnified manyfold.

This is all by way of saying that the obsessive nature of the creative person is not a bad thing in and of itself, as it allows him to productively obsess about his work. But when that powerful obsessive nature gets a grip on drinking or using as its favorite way to alleviate anxiety, that grip is often an iron one.

CREATIVE-RECOVERY JOURNAL QUESTION

How would you characterize the relationship between anxiety and addiction?

The Intertwining of Issues

Consider rock musicians as one class of creative person at high risk for addiction. This high risk was recently underscored in a statistical study from the British researcher Mark Bellis, who indicated that both English and American rock and pop stars were more than twice as likely to die prematurely as were ordinary citizens of the same age. For rock musicians, in addition to all the reasons that might incline anyone toward an addiction, the following factors pile on.

Creative-Identity Issues

1. Many rock musicians love highs with a special love and initially start using their drug of choice (or all drugs) to get a buzz on, to socialize, to

loosen up, to have fun, to party, and to live the life of sex, drugs, and rock and roll.

2. Many rock musicians possess a belief system in which rebellion and nonconformity are highly valued. The rebellious mind-set of the rock musician causes him to thumb his nose at conventional ideas of moderation and to act out with drugs and alcohol.

3. Many rock musicians are influenced by myths and stereotypes of what it means to be a rock musician. Drinking hard and taking drugs are badges of honor and ways of conforming to the image of the rock musician, and they relish the idea of being a bad boy or a bad girl.

4. Many rock musicians, like all people, suffer from anxiety issues; additionally, they may be burdened by performance-anxiety problems. Their addiction is rooted in the common human experience of anxiety and may also be rooted in the special performer's problem of stage fright.

5. Many rock musicians, especially as they start to have fans, get swelled heads, which leads to ego-attachment problems such as narcissism, grandiosity, and arrogance, all of which play a part in helping them deny that their using has become a problem.

6. Many rock musicians expend an enormous amount of adrenaline when they perform, and their bodies are saturated with adrenaline when they finish. High on adrenaline, they find it hard to come down and as a consequence take drugs and alcohol to help them deal with the adrenaline coursing through their system.

Creative-Environment Issues

1. Many rock musicians frequent bars and clubs, play music in bars and clubs, and live a life that revolves around bars and clubs. They are around drugs and alcohol more than other people and are embedded in

a culture where drug experimentation is the norm and alcohol and drugs are regularly gifted on them.

2. Many rock musicians live on the fringes of society, where it is more acceptable to engage in illicit activities. They even pride themselves on living on the fringe; engaging in these illicit activities becomes a source of satisfaction.

3. Many rock musicians are poor (unless they become rich and then have different risk factors). Poor people suffer more day-to-day frustrations than do their middle-class counterparts, and they use drugs and alcohol to help themselves forget about their poverty and their misery. Rich rock musicians, on the other hand, are often shielded from the natural consequences of their addictive behavior by hangers-on or people who work for them, a situation that enables them to keep using until they have life-threatening problems. Either way, rock musicians do drugs and alcohol in part because of the challenges of their socioeconomic class.

4. Many rock musicians experience life as a continual party, since the activity of making music excites and loosens up the people around them and causes a party to erupt spontaneously. As it is customary for drinks and drugs to start flowing at parties, this perpetual party life produces a perpetual environment of drugs and alcohol.

5. Rock musicians are surrounded by other rock musicians who are likely to possess the same addictive tendencies, outsider mind-set, and lifestyle myths that they do. They are bound to feel pressured to use by virtue of the activities and blandishments of their peers.

You can see how a rock musician who is troubled by an addiction has a complex, intertwined set of issues with which she must deal. She must deal with the ideas, opinions, and myths in her own head, with her coursing energy and adrenaline, with the addictive nature of her companions, and with the way that drinks and drugs surround her at every turn. This is really too much to handle without the iron sword of commitment and the armor of a complete recovery program.

Even if you're not a rock musician, the same sort of issues with identity and environment can contribute to your own risks for addiction. As these issues multiply, your risk is compounded. Since issues such as these exist for all creative people, whatever your art form or profession, you are likely to find yourself confronted by some number of these influential additional risks.

CREATIVE-RECOVERY JOURNAL QUESTIONS

1. What choices have you made—for instance, to work in a high-pressure job where alcohol flows freely or to associate with exciting people who do drugs as a matter of course—that put you at risk for addiction? List as many of these choices as you can.

2. Do you nurture positive beliefs about the use of substances or mind-altering behaviors and tend to minimize or deny any negative consequences to their use? List as many of the cognitions that support your addictive tendencies as you can identify.

3. What puts you at the *most* risk for addiction? Is it your biological inheritance, your childhood troubles, your creative nature, or your career choice to write or to paint? If you had to choose one of the many risk factors we've discussed, which one would it be—and why?

4. Try to identify as many risk factors as pertain to you. (Given all that we've discussed, this list may be quite long.) For each pertinent

risk factor, answer the following question: Do you believe that this constitutes a small risk, a medium risk, or a large risk?

5. How can you minimize these risks in your life? What can you do right now to minimize these risks?

CREATIVE-RECOVERY EXERCISES

1. If you agree that as a creative person you have a certain added pressure, energy, or ambition inside you, describe how that pressure, energy, or ambition is itself a risk for addiction. Make this as creative an exploration as you like and involve your writing skills, your visual arts skills, your scientific skills, your musical skills, or any other skill that will help you describe for yourself how these added internal pressures amount to significant added risk.

2. Think about your particular creative group: all painters, all poets, all magicians, and so on. What are the special risks for addiction that come with that territory? Articulate the characteristic risks for addiction that members of your group face, maybe by using the characteristic tools of that medium: by painting to portray the risks that painters face, by composing to portray the special risks that composers face, and so on.

Risk Awareness

In this chapter and the previous one we've looked at many risk factors. The only real question is, to what extent are you personally at risk? Of course you can't make an exact calculation or an infallible prediction. But you can think through the issues we've presented: your family history of addiction, the extent to which you were unable to form secure attachments in childhood, the environmental stressors peculiar to your profession, the risks posed by your creative nature and your need to assert your individuality, and so on.

Before we move on, it is time to assess your own risk. You can do it in the whimsical way we presented at the beginning of the chapter, by trying to assign a percentage to each risk and creating a playful pie chart of your personal risk. Or you might try to do it in a narrative way by writing an essay-length piece in which you chat with yourself about your particular risk picture. The goal of this self-analysis is, first, to help you identify your personal-risk picture and, second, to familiarize you with the reality of risk. Please spend some real time engaging this culminating exercise.

Creative Exercises

The theme for this chapter's creative exercises is developmental, environmental, and creative-nature risk assessment for addiction. As before, we encourage you to fully engage your creative nature by expanding beyond your comfort zone and experimenting with all the genres.

Notice what thoughts or feelings get in the way and which spur you forward. When you are finished with each exercise, make notes in your creative-recovery journal about your various responses to doing the exercises and what you have learned about your developmental, environmental, and creative-nature risks for addiction.

1. For the writer in you

Create some character sketches where each character has a prominent—but different—risk factor for addiction. Describe a character whose biology set him or her up, one whose childhood or teenage experiences set the character up, and another whose adult environment was the setup. Whom do you most identify with in these scenarios? Whom do you love or hate? Whom do you find yourself wanting to blame or protect?

2. For the visual artist in you

Draw several portraits of a person at different stages of his or her life: as a child living through a difficult childhood, as an adolescent living through a difficult adolescence, as a young adult living through a difficult adulthood, and as a mature adult in recovery. Ask yourself the same questions as in the previous exercise. Which portrait has the strongest impact on you? Which was easier or most difficult to render?

3. For the actor in you

You are auditioning for the role of someone who was harmed in childhood but is not in touch with those experiences, someone who, if questioned, would vehemently deny that those experiences ever happened. How would you portray this character? What would be the most challenging aspect of the role for you? What would be the easiest?

4. For the scientist in you

What might be the operational definitions of a biological risk factor, a developmental risk factor, an environmental risk factor, and a creative-nature risk factor? How would you measure or quantify these risk factors? Which would be the hardest to measure? Why?

5. For the dreamer in you

Imagine that you possess multiple risk factors for addiction. If you could eliminate just one, which would it be? Why? What would be different afterward? What would stay the same?

Postscript

We hope that you are getting the hang of this self-assessment process using your natural creativity. What have you learned so far about your personal-risk factors for getting addicted? Which of these risk factors can you modify and which need to be accepted and responsibly managed? Try to answer these questions before proceeding on to the next chapter, where we'll help you assess your current level of addictive use by describing the abuse continuum.

3   *The Abuse Continuum*

How do you conceptualize your alcohol use? Your Internet surfing? Your riskier behaviors, such as gambling, breakneck driving, or reckless sex? When a behavior of yours possesses both positive and negative consequences—for instance, that you enjoy your drug high but not the morning after or that you love the excitement of a gambling spree but not the financial difficulties that follow—how do you weigh whether the behavior is more positive or more negative? How do you judge whether one of your behaviors can be safely continued or ought to be modified or curtailed?

For some, even their obsessive creating falls into the category of a behavior whose negative consequences need to be evaluated. Many creative people worry about whether working so feverishly at their art, to the exclusion of the rest of their life, isn't as much a negative as a positive. In this chapter we'd like to help you think more clearly about how to evaluate the riskiness of your behaviors.

When people begin to experiment with mind-altering substances or behaviors, they generally expect a number of things to happen. They expect to feel better quickly; to relax; to have fun; to fit into a social scene; to become momentarily enlightened, passionate, or brave; or to escape painful thoughts or feelings for a while. Creative people often expect these behaviors to enhance their creativity or solidify their identity as a creative person. The one thing that they *never* expect is that they will become alcoholics, drug addicts, sex addicts, shopping addicts, or gambling addicts. This is true even for those of us who grew up surrounded by addicted family members and who might have gotten some early clues about our increased vulnerability to addiction.

"It will never happen to me" is a frequent refrain heard among addicts and one that Dr. Claudia Black popularized after she began working with adult children of alcoholics. We do not expect to become anything like the disturbing characters we've seen portrayed as stereotypical end-stage alcoholics or addicts in the movies, such as Ray Milland in *The Lost Weekend,* Jack Lemmon and Lee Remick in *Days of Wine and Roses,* Meg Ryan in *When a Man Loves a Woman,* Sandra Bullock in *28 Days,* or Nicholas Cage in *Leaving Las Vegas.* We do not expect to experience extreme negative consequences from our use or to lose control of ourselves. How, then, does this happen? How does the casual use of soothing substances or behaviors develop into the heartbreaking, compulsive problem we understand as addiction?

The Abuse Continuum

In recent years the addictions field and the science behind it have grown and changed enormously. Some controversies have been settled, and new ones have developed to take their place. Emerging information on addiction and on brain functioning promises new understanding and treatment options. By employing harm-reduction and motivational-enhancement strategies, clinicians have gotten better at helping clients "where they are" rather than expecting them to have already changed.

If you are blocked trying to figure out the ending to your first novel, that is exactly where you are; you can't be expected to know what a novelist with ten novels under his belt knows about how to break that block. Similarly, if you are stuck abusing alcohol, you can't be expected to understand how recovery is going to work; rather, you have to be helped—and maybe coaxed—into recovery, so that in recovery you can acquire the actual experience of recovery. This is all by way of saying that people are exactly where they are—including exactly where they are along the abuse continuum—and they need to be met there by a clinician, a sponsor, a friend, or whomever. This also means that you need the self-awareness and patience to meet yourself where you are. If you are already chemically dependent, it makes no sense to wish that you were only a habitual user: you or both you and your clinician have to deal with your precise reality.

To those of us in the field who hear countless stories about people's relationships with mind-altering substances or with addictive behaviors such as gambling or compulsive sex, predictable levels of use emerge. It is common for people to enter and exit different levels depending on life circumstances, sometimes fluidly and rapidly moving up and down the abuse continuum. However, once a person has graduated to the dependence level of use, she will invariably return to that level if she continues actively using, a point that we want to underline at the outset.

The following are the levels of use found along the abuse continuum:

Abstinence. You do not use a given addictive substance or engage in a given addictive behavior at all. (This stage obviously does not apply in the same sense for something like a food addiction, where abstinence would amount to starvation. In that case, abstinence refers to maintaining a healthy diet.)

Experimentation. At the experimentation level, you have limited exposure to a given addictive substance or behavior. You may experiment with a substance out of curiosity or peer influence, but you do not continue to use. Experimentation rarely results in serious negative consequences, and if you do experience some negative consequences, you discontinue use accordingly.

Social use. Your use of a particular substance or your engagement in a particular behavior is infrequent, does not establish an ongoing pattern, does not have substantial impact on your life, and is primarily recreational in nature. Social users take the initiative to use and, unlike experimenters, anticipate a known desired effect. It's like the difference between experimenting with watercolors and not finding it to your liking versus returning to watercolors every once in a while because you like the risky experience of having to deal with colors that drip.

Habitual use. With habitual use you have established a regular pattern of use and you are now, at least to some extent, controlled by the substance. Some people stay at this level without negative consequences and further progression. There is both a clear positive sense and a clear negative sense to having put a habit in place: getting in the habit of working on your novel every day is a good thing if you intend to write, but getting into the concurrent habit of relaxing after you write with a few beers is less clearly a pure positive, especially depending on your personal-risk factors for moving from this innocent-enough habit to abuse or dependence.

Abuse. At this level you experience clear negative consequences of your use but continue to use anyway. The negative consequences can be obviously use related (such as a DUI arrest) and difficult (but not impossible) to deny, or more subtle (such as feeling chronically unmotivated in response to a marijuana habit). In the latter case, if your goal is to continue using, you have a golden opportunity to misattribute that consequence to something other than the use. For example, you can blame your lack of motivation on your lousy job. This is how denial typically works at the abuse level: you admit to certain consequences but are reluctant to connect the dots back to the cause, your now-abusive use of a substance or engagement in a behavior.

Dependence. Becoming dependent means that you've experienced a compulsive loss of control related to your use in addition to all the negative consequences of using. Typically, the addictive substance or behavior has become the organizing principle in your life, pushing other people or activities, including your creative efforts, to the sidelines.

The more you pay attention to the distinctions that these six stops on the abuse continuum represent, the better you will be able to prevent a slide down the continuum or, if you have already slid into abuse and dependence, the better you will be able to climb back up. To begin with, think about these six words and phrases: abstinence, experimentation, social use, habitual use, abuse, and dependence. Each is rich, interesting, and resonant and should pique your creative imagination. Does abstinence have the same meaning when it's applied to not using heroin, not having sex, or not going to the mall to shop? When is daily Internet surfing more like a not-too-worrisome habit, more like abuse, and more like dependence? Spend a little time thinking through these distinctions.

Look back on your life and pick out three potentially risky behaviors—for example, it might be your alcohol use, your marijuana use, and your sports gambling—and describe your connection to each one in terms of these six categories. Try to do a deep, sophisticated, and creative job, letting in all the subtleties. For instance, consider how you may have abstained from trying something because you suspected that it was your drug of choice and experimenting with it would have sent you right to dependence. Your examination of these six stops along the abuse continuum is an opportunity to use your creative imagination in pursuit of insights about your addiction issues.

If you want to go a further step in your examination, consider the following. There are many theories about how people get addicted. We subscribe to what has been called the bio-psycho-social model of addiction as the best integration of current theories, though we add a spiritual, or existential, component. What this means practically will become clearer as we proceed, but as shorthand it means that addiction involves biological, psychological, social, and spiritual or existential factors in dynamic interaction. Repeat the last exercise, where you examined three of your potentially risky behaviors, and see if you can identify where on the abuse continuum they have taken you and also what dynamics—biological, psychological, social, and spiritual or existential—might have been at play.

Using Your Creative Nature

You can use your creative nature to help deal with your addictive tendencies and analyze your situation, including where you fall on the abuse continuum with respect to any substance or behavior. Consider Mary's story:

I have an addictive personality. And although I'm not "using" anything nowadays, I really don't think I've resolved my addictive tendencies. I've merely replaced destructive addictions with more productive behaviors that still have that "addictive" edge to them—like the obsessive way I paint.

Twenty-three years ago I handled the demise of my first marriage by smoking pot and watching television. At my lowest point, my day consisted of going to work, coming home, overeating, smoking pot, and sometimes drinking. Oh, and I was a smoker too!

Finally I began to fight the addictions. First went the pot. I liked it better than booze, but my new husband had four children and I figured that I needed to learn to live without illegal substances. The pot smoking was replaced by crafts making.

Then, fifteen years ago, I started painting. From the first day of class I was hooked. Every day I would get up at 3:00 A.M. and paint before work. That was becoming my new addiction—and I was happy about it. Indeed, I'm still on a modified version of that first schedule.

I was still drinking every day, but I could sense that the painting was helping me get ready to quit the drinking. I would drink and feel terrible the next day and have trouble getting to the painting, and that became the tipping point. I started a real recovery program, in the service of my painting, and it actually made it easy to quit. I had one slip eight years ago—one drink—and nothing since. I replaced drinking with painting.

Cigarettes were another story. I painted and smoked at the same time. (Really smart around turpentine!) Then one day I bought a piano and started playing the piano again. It may sound funny, but I ended up replacing cigarettes with the piano. Not smoking really took some adjusting and perseverance, and I still chew gum during my first painting session. But I don't smoke anymore.

I continue to struggle with food. It's been my toughest battle. However, I've returned to writing and have no doubt that it will eventually replace my need to overeat. As for the television work that I do, producing my own cable television show somehow helps me with recovery in a broad sense. I've really come a long way. It's hard to believe there was a time when I wasn't painting, writing, playing the piano, or producing my own show. The way I see it, I am hardwired with addictive tendencies. I am so grateful that now I funnel them toward creation rather than destruction.

Mary was successful because she was able to use her creative nature in her recovery. As a creative person, you have an innate set of skills that you can bring to the work of recovery. What aspects of your creative nature can you bring to bear to help in this process of self-examination? All of the following:

You can think. Not every creative act is an act of pure cogitation, but thinking is a core creative skill. What were creative scientists and social scientists like Newton, Einstein, Freud, and Jung doing? Or painters like Picasso and Matisse or composers like Bach and Beethoven? They had ideas and they used their native thinking ability to analyze, synthesize, evaluate, and integrate ideas in the service of their creative interests.

Thinking is a much more difficult enterprise than people imagine because it requires that we really stop, get internally quiet, endure the anxiety that not knowing provokes, and more. That's why deep thinking is difficult and most people avoid doing it. But you have the ability to think available to you, and you can decide to deal with your addiction thoughtfully. That is part of your creative nature. Right now, take a few minutes and use this core ability to help better understand where you fall on the abuse continuum with respect to the substances and behaviors that give you the most trouble. Start to think about your addiction in an intelligent and realistic way.

You can innovate. You have the ability to operate in new ways, to turn what you've learned from experience into new thoughts, new approaches, new plans, and new products. You may not produce one earthshaking invention after another like an Edison, but you can orchestrate a song or, at a higher level of innovation, create a new way of being that excludes harmful substances and behaviors but still includes meaning and joy.

It is true that on most days you may not attempt anything particularly innovative and may only accomplish one routine thing after another. But your ability to innovate is nevertheless within you. It is a core feature of your creative nature, and you can enlist it to help with your recovery. Right now, take a few minutes and dream up an innovative way to make some important change in your life—maybe the change from abuse or dependence to abstinence? For example, if you are a dancer, you might turn the twelve steps of Alcoholics Anonymous into a modern dance and feel the power of the steps as you dance them, translating "mere words" into a full-body experience. This is the essence of innovation.

You can imagine. You can picture scenes in your mind's eye. You can dream, both in the nighttime sense and in the sense of cherishing hopes and envisioning goals. You can imagine the future one way, with you still drinking alcoholically, and you can imagine the future another way, with you sober. You can imagine what it would be like to paint your living room Chinese red, and you can imagine what it would be like to live a disciplined life rather than an undisciplined life: there is really nothing that you can't imagine.

Currently you may do little daydreaming and imagining, but that ability is nevertheless available to you. It is a core feature of your creative nature, and it allows you to picture a future to which you might want to aspire. Right now, spend a few minutes imagining yourself moving from abuse or dependence to abstinence. Picture that movement in your mind's eye: how your apartment would look without drug paraphernalia around, how your evenings would look if you weren't hunting for a fix, how your art would look with you paying more sober attention to it.

You can problem solve. You have the ability to conceptualize problems and to arrive at solutions to problems. You do this all the time, whether it's prioritizing your tasks at work, managing your money, or deciding what to do to help your aging parents. Not only can you solve problems but you also have the ability to recognize that there is a problem to solve, whether that problem is the lackluster ending to your novel or your drinking ways.

Likewise, you can construe your life as a project requiring you to solve one problem after another. Creative recovery makes use of exactly this talent: you recognize that some of your friends, hangouts, and behaviors may be problematic—and then you solve those problems. Right now, choose as the problem to solve some recognition you've had as a result of reading thus far—and solve it. It may be the knottiest problem you will ever face, like taking the long journey from dependence to abstinence, but you are a born problem solver.

Maybe you're noticing that you're spending far too many hours at the local casino playing blackjack. If you treat your gambling as a problem rather than as a pastime, you can begin to identify your own solutions, for example, by deciding to experience the adrenaline rush you crave from your creative efforts rather than from winning big pots.

You can manifest your personality strengths. You have the ability to make use of your curiosity, your confidence, your courage, and the many other important personality traits that you possess. When you are at your most curious, most confident, most courageous, and so on—when you are at your liveliest and your best—you create as a matter of course.

An idea for a novel arises because you are curious; because you are confident, you feel equal to writing it; because you are manifesting your courage, you stick with it.

Exactly the same is true with respect to recovery. When you manifest the traits that you already possess—your empathy, your honesty, your ability to concentrate, your thoughtfulness, your playfulness, your resiliency, and so on—you put yourself squarely on the road to recovery. Take a minute to list your personality strengths—it will amount to a long list, if you are patient—and think through how each quality on that list could be mustered to help you move in the right direction along the abuse continuum, away from abuse and dependence and toward abstinence.

You can minimize your weaknesses. Sometimes you feel very anxious and can't seem to do anything about it, and other times you manage to quell your feelings of anxiety by the way you talk to yourself and reframe the situation. Sometimes you feel the need to lash out at people, and other times you notice what you're about to do and stop yourself from making the situation worse. This ability to manage our shadows, shortfalls, and weaknesses is what allows an anxious actor to still perform, a disgruntled inventor to still invent, and a morose writer to still write.

No one does a perfect job of minimizing his or her weaknesses, but each of us has the ability to notice our shortcomings and do something about them. This ability is as vital to the recovery process as it is to the creative process. Make a list of your weaknesses—this, too, may be a long list—and think through how you might minimize each one of them during the recovery process. Also, try to determine which of these weaknesses may be implicated in your having landed at a place along the abuse continuum where you don't want to be.

You can hold a single ambitious idea over time. One of the attributes that distinguish a creative person from her uncreative peers is that she believes that she can do something exceptional like write an excellent novel or grow a complicated business, and then she can hold that idea in a productively obsessed way over long stretches of time. We all have that ability, but most of us use it only rarely, maybe to help get through a training program or a graduate-school course or to lose weight for an upcoming high school reunion.

Still, as rarely as we use it, each of us has experienced holding an ambitious idea in mind for six months or a year at a time, and the fact that we have done it once is proof that we can do it again. This time you will want to enlist this core ability in the service of your recovery. Your ambitious idea is that you can be sober *and* creative, and you will want to hold on to that idea every hour of every day for the rest of your life. That is ambitious—but absolutely within your grasp.

You can engage in an ongoing practice. As an artist, you are able to maintain a mindful practice in which you return in a regular, sustained way to a particular project or a certain way of being. It is in the repertoire of creative people to pay systematic attention to their beliefs and their intentions by setting aside periods of time (or even a whole life) committed to consciously quieting their mind, separating themselves from their everyday distractions, and focusing on what they consider to be of most importance to them, whether that be their novel, their painting, or their quilting.

Part of your creative nature is your ability to create and sustain a mindful practice in support of your recovery, a practice that resembles the practice of someone engaged in daily yoga, instrument practice, or art making. Approach your recovery as regularly and attentively as you approach your art. We will go into this idea in more detail in later chapters, as we invite you to begin your own morning mindfulness practice and your own creativity practice. For now, reflect on the idea that constructing and maintaining an ongoing practice is part of your repertoire as a creative person.

You can become present. Most people find it hard to bring their whole being to the present moment. Instead, they rush from one thing to the next or distract themselves with the noise provided by media, the Internet, and the everyday swirl of errands and gossip—or by their addiction. Rather than becoming present, they hypnotize themselves with the vicarious reality of television, brood about the past, fantasize about the future, or drink alcoholically.

Creative people know that it is part of their nature to quietly bring their complete being into the present moment for the sake of awareness and mindfulness. Your creative nature provides the ability to be really present for the sake of your novel or your scientific research—or your sobriety. We will provide strategies and tools for becoming more present shortly, but for now simply imagine what it would be like to be so present that you suddenly understood that you were abusing a substance, surrendered to the fact that you had a serious problem, and committed to change. That experience of real presence is available to you.

You can become passionate. Passion is a large element of your creative nature. It is love, ardor, or passion that fuels the creative journey and permits a person to deal with the many difficulties inherent in the creative act. Without loving music, it would be too hard to compose a symphony; without loving discovering how things work, it would be too frustrating to try out thousands of versions of your lightbulb before arriving at the secret of the tungsten filament.

Without manifesting passion on your own behalf, a passion to be your best self and rise to the occasion, it is hard to be bothered with recovering.

That passion is available to you; the trick is to fall in love with recovery. For now, think of the difference between the following two states: wanting to move along the abuse continuum in the right direction and *passionately* wanting to make that movement. Can you feel the difference?

You can devote yourself to an ideal. As a creative person you believe that contributing a strong novel or a new vaccine is meaningful and important to the general good of the world. This belief is part of your creative nature. You see yourself as working in the humanist or humanitarian tradition, and your creative efforts are not just expressions of ego or the means to fame but the way you manifest your principles and live authentically.

You can use that same innate creative ability to devote yourself to an ideal by raising sobriety to an ideal. Devotion to an ideal is not the only motivational force in our being, but it is one of the most powerful. Think of how many millions of people have given up their lives for an ideal: you can use that same power to save yours.

This way of presenting what your innate creative nature means may surprise you. You may have been expecting something about special talents, divine inspiration, or qualities such as eccentricity and nonconformity— something that looks more like a crazy artist or a mad scientist. But this unromantic picture is the truth about our creative nature. We are creative when we manifest these eleven qualities; no amount of eccentricity, wildness, or romantic fervor can serve as substitutes.

You possess all eleven of these innate abilities, but you may not be accessing them or manifesting them as much as you would like. We've worked with thousands of creative individuals, and it is our observation that the regularly creative ones are more thoughtful, are more passionate, permit themselves more ambitious projects . . . that is, they do a better job of manifesting these eleven elements. The more you manage to manifest these eleven elements, the more creative you will become and the better position you will find yourself in to accurately locate yourself along the abuse continuum and to opt for recovery.

CREATIVE-RECOVERY EXERCISE

Choose one of the traits described above to examine deeply. Employ your art discipline or a discipline you want to experiment with and discern what becoming present, devoting yourself to an ideal, or one of the other traits means to you. Pick a trait that you intuit is going to serve you well in the recovery process and then examine it in poetry, watercolor, song, or in some other creative way.

The Case of Joan

In the following case study you'll see how a creative client in therapy is helped to use her natural thinking ability and her natural problem-solving ability to deal with a drinking problem that has arisen out of the blue, a problem that is not so far progressed that she needs to institute a complete recovery program.

When Joan J. came to see Susan, she complained of depression—which she explained had recently struck for the first time in her life—as well as uncharacteristic bouts of anger. Susan learned that Joan was a healthy forty-five-year-old married woman, a real estate agent, and a part-time craftsperson who had been with her husband for twenty years. She had no history of psychiatric care and no family history of addiction. She had a young adult son who was in college in another state.

In the previous two years she had gone from drinking on occasion—on the order of a glass of wine about three times a month—to drinking several glasses of wine several times a week. About once a month for the past six months she had drunk enough on the weekend to result in angry outbursts—on one occasion at a dinner party in front of friends. At that point her husband, who was not a big drinker, expressed some real concern. That expression of concern, coupled with her own embarrassment, caused her to make a therapy appointment.

Joan described a long-standing history of problem-free, social alcohol use that had evolved into habitual alcohol use two years before and was crossing over into abuse as she drank more frequently and consumed more. Whereas she'd previously spent her free time after work in her studio working on crafts projects, recently she'd started to rely on a cocktail hour instead. Much to her chagrin, she found that drinking regularly only reduced her motivation to work in her studio.

Even as negative consequences of her use became apparent to her and those around her, she continued to drink. She eventually enrolled in Susan's three-month early-recovery group and stopped drinking entirely without any obvious turmoil, and over the course of those three months her situation became clearer.

With the emotional support and structure of the group, she was able to identify the impetus behind the change in her drinking pattern. She became aware of using alcohol to mask deep-seated resentments toward her husband. Over the years, he had relocated the family repeatedly without consulting her, each time disrupting her real estate business and her fledgling crafts business. She came to see a general pattern of feeling controlled and uncared for by him. These feelings became more obvious after her son left home, leaving her alone with her husband. Joan was mad at her husband and mad at herself for repeatedly swallowing her anger to avoid the inevitable conflict that would have ensued.

The outcome of this case was that Joan got educated about addiction, took a break from her drinking, and initiated marital counseling to solve her problem with her husband. She learned to communicate her feelings directly and to take care of herself in effective ways. In addition to more productive thinking and problem solving, she tapped back into her creative strengths by picturing a better relationship with her husband, improving her weak communication skills, and increasing her support to minimize her fear of interpersonal conflict.

Joan returned to her regular practice of crafts making, reminding herself what a central part of her overall self-care making art really was. She saw how discontinuing her crafts practice had been a self-defeating method of expressing resentment toward her husband and passionately recommitted herself to her creative efforts. She vowed to stay authentically connected to her real feelings at any cost and to actively cocreate her part of a satisfying marriage.

After three months of sobriety in the group, continued therapeutic support, and healthier communication in her marriage, Joan eventually returned to social drinking without problems. She understood that if she found herself drinking more heavily again or experienced problems related to her alcohol use, she would get help and seriously consider abstinence.

The Case of Frank

In this second case study we see how a client who is much further along the abuse continuum can reclaim core creative qualities and employ them for the sake of recovery.

Frank G. was court ordered to chemical-dependency treatment following his arrest for selling methamphetamine. He was thirty-five years old, divorced, and with three small children whom, as a consequence of his drug use, he saw under supervised conditions. He was employed as a construction foreman for a large company but had shown some promise doing spoken word performance in his community before his drug use took over.

Frank's paternal grandfather was alcoholic, and his parents divorced when he was a small child. He and his younger brother subsequently lived with their mother, with no paternal contact. Frank began using marijuana and alcohol at the age of fourteen. He was exposed to rap, hip-hop music, and poetry and eventually started doing spoken word performances for his friends. He had aspirations to be an artist.

By sixteen Frank had been suspended from high school twice for drug use. By eighteen he was using methamphetamine on a regular basis, demonstrating an abuse pattern. By the time he was twenty-five, he'd lost two jobs as well as his wife as a consequence of his drug use. He continued using. Poetry and spoken word performance were long gone, as were his artistic aspirations.

Frank reported that prior to his arrest he had been engaged in a binge pattern of speed use, using increasing quantities, primarily on the weekends. He tried to recuperate during the week by limiting his intake to a few beers daily. He reported various attempts to control his use over the years, alternating with renewed denial that he had a problem.

Frank jumped onto the use continuum running, moving into habitual use almost immediately. His risk factors for becoming substance dependent were high on all counts—genetic vulnerability, adverse childhood experiences, and initiation of use in early adolescence, before his brain had finished developing. He began showing the negative consequences of substance abuse by the time he was in his twenties but nevertheless continued to use.

By the time he was court ordered into treatment, Frank was clearly alcohol and methamphetamine dependent, showing ongoing loss of control over his use. For Frank, abstinence and staying in treatment were the immediate recovery goals. Half measures were not going to prove sufficient for someone in Frank's situation. At his location on the abuse continuum, unless he managed to get a complete recovery program in place, the likelihood was great that his addiction would prove his ruin.

This goal was met in part by enlisting Frank's personality strengths, including his resiliency, his stubbornness (now enlisted on the side of sobriety rather than addiction), his optimism, his ability to imagine (by having him visualize a sober future and a return to the world of poetry and spoken word), and his desire to devote himself to an ideal (to the ideal of becoming a good parent to his three small children). Because he had these core skills available to him, as does every creative person, over the course of a lengthy treatment regimen Frank was able to enter shaky but real early recovery.

CREATIVE-RECOVERY JOURNAL QUESTIONS

It is time to think through your history of use. List all of your problematic behaviors (for example, overeating, gambling, and so forth) and all the potentially addictive substances you've used. For each one, answer the following questions:

1. How long have you been engaging in this behavior or using this substance?
2. How often do you engage in this behavior or use this substance?
3. What negative consequences have you experienced from engaging in this behavior or using this substance? For example, has your use hurt you emotionally, physically, socially, occupationally, legally, or spiritually?
4. How have you responded to these negative consequences? Did you continue using or behaving that way despite negative consequences?
5. Have you experienced a loss of control related to your use? Have you repeatedly continued to use after you told yourself that you would stop, or used more than you told yourself you would?
6. Has the mind-altering substance or problematic behavior become more important to you than most other aspects of your life?
7. Look back at the criteria used to distinguish one step from another along the abuse continuum. For each substance or behavior on your list, make your best educated guess as to where you fall on the continuum, making subtle distinctions between social use and habitual use and between abuse and dependence.
8. Draw a red flag next to each behavior or substance that you feel falls into the habitual use, abuse, or dependence categories.
9. Make the following simple pledge with respect to each of your red-flag items: "I am going to pay attention to this." As we proceed, we'll describe the sort of attention we believe you ought to pay.

Sometimes we completely abstain from using a dangerous substance or engaging in a dangerous behavior. Sometimes we only experiment. Sometimes we use socially and recreationally. Sometimes we move into the graver areas of habitual use, abuse, and dependence. As a creative person, you possess the tools to evaluate your place along the abuse continuum with respect to any substance or behavior that threatens you. We hope that you have now begun that evaluation and that you will continue that evaluation using the following exercises.

Creative Exercises

We invite you now to continue your courageous and unflinching look at where you stand in two important areas: where you are on the abuse continuum by virtue of your behaviors with mind-altering substances or activities, and how you are utilizing the essential qualities of your creative nature. We'll borrow some advice from the twelve-step programs in suggesting that you "don't exaggerate and don't minimize" your patterns. Honest appraisal will serve you well whether or not you are prepared to make changes at this time.

This chapter's creative exercises are designed to help you assess where you are in these two areas. To review, the points along the abuse continuum include abstinence, experimentation, social use, habitual use, abuse, and dependence. Feel free to review the eleven aspects of your creative nature that were previously outlined. As you do the exercises, notice your responses. Are these exercises getting more difficult or easier to do as you proceed with more information? As before, take note of your attitudes, emotional responses, and motivations in response to the exercises. Keep going, adding these responses to your creative-recovery journal.

1. For the writer in you

Write a short story in which several people on different places along the abuse continuum interact at a large party. What do you notice? Describe the attitudes and actions personifying the characters in each of the stages you've chosen. How do your characters respond to one another? Would this change if it were a small, intimate party instead of a large, crowded party? How does this story end? Which character best utilizes the qualities of his or her creative nature? Which character most represents you?

2. For the visual artist in you

Draw or paint the stage you've identified with on the abuse continuum: abstinence, experimentation, social use, habitual use, abuse, or dependence. What materials will you need for this piece? How large an image do you envision? How well would this image share space with other images? Is there any inherent action or is it stagnant? Look at your drawing or painting. How do you feel about being in your place on the abuse continuum? Would others have identified your place the same way? If not, why not?

3. For the actor in you

Imagine playing a drunk who never looks drunk. Then imagine playing a drunk who *thinks* that he never looks drunk. How would they differ? How would the audience tend to react to these different characters? Which character do you most want to play and why? Do these characters demonstrate skills and qualities of a creative nature? If so, which ones?

4. For the musician in you

Pick out a few of your best creative qualities and compose or play a piece that describes them. Experiment with whatever musical form, instruments, genre, tempo, and mood you feel that you need here. When you have finished, describe the piece you composed or played. Now add some lyrics to this piece that identify where you are on the abuse continuum. Think about how you can use your creative qualities to help you take the next step toward recovery, if you need to.

5. For the dreamer in you

Imagine a more creative you. What creative-nature skills and qualities would you want to increase to achieve this version of yourself? What obstacles in your life would you need to remove to get to the more creative you? For example, is your current place on the abuse continuum one of these obstacles?

Postscript

Consider what you have observed and learned about your place on the abuse continuum and about how well you are utilizing the qualities and skills associated with your true creative nature. While we encourage you to give yourself credit for what you are already doing right, chances are that you have found room for improvement. Keep reading, as the next chapter, "Accepting the Call to Change" is a call to action.

PART TWO

Working

4 ⬙ *Accepting the Call to Change*

Sometimes we need to make a big change, even though we feel unequal to the attempt and are scared of the consequences. Novelist and diarist Anaïs Nin described this darkly uncomfortable situation beautifully when she said: "And then the day came when the risk to remain tight in a bud was more painful than the risk it took to blossom." If you have addiction issues, then you will also have change issues, as there are behavioral changes and psychological changes that you will need to make—and making them is unlikely to prove easy.

Think of the kinds of big changes that may have confronted you in your creative life. How easy was it to accept that your novel, the one you'd spent two years on, needed a complete overhaul if it was to be readable? How easy was it to change your research focus, the one you'd invested a decade in, even though you could see that you were heading in a dead-end direction? In each case you may have known—even known for certain—that the change was needed, but how long did it take you to make that change . . . if you made it at all?

What exactly gets in the way of our making needed changes? Imagine the dancer who sees the handwriting on the wall and knows that her professional dance career is ending because she is in too much pain to continue dancing. She carries on by dint of will and by ingesting lots of pain medication, but she knows that she should open up her heart and her mind to her next life stage. Why not gracefully make the change—and end the pain? Because she still loves to dance, because it makes her incredibly sad to imagine not dancing, because she dreamed of doing great things as a dancer and hasn't accomplished them yet, because she doubts that she will ever feel alive again if she doesn't get to dance, because she has no idea what to do next and can see only the void looming, and because of other powerful reasons just as real and just as pressing as these. That's a lot!

She isn't ready to make the change—not by a long shot. In the child-development field, "readiness" is a technical term: an infant isn't ready to run, a toddler isn't ready to ride a bicycle, a first-grader usually isn't ready for calculus. The child simply can't do the thing yet. However, when we say that an adult isn't ready to do something, we have a different definition in mind: we mean that he could do it but he doesn't want to do it, he's unwilling to do it, he's not motivated to do it. That's the sense in which addicts aren't ready to get sober.

You may know that you have addiction issues and even know that they are causing you severe difficulties, and yet you may not be ready to change. Given all the reasons that a person has for holding on to a love—and addiction is a kind of love—the fact that you may not be ready to change isn't really all that surprising. Think of some big change that you knew you needed to make but that, for the longest time, you simply couldn't make. What got in the way of your making that change? Those inner obstacles to change are what concern us in this chapter.

The Five Stages of Change

There are many ways to think about change and the obstacles to change. We'd like to present one model, a model that the addiction researchers

James Prochaska and Carlo DiClemente and their colleagues have been re-searching for more than twenty years. Based on their observations of indi-viduals dealing with a variety of addictive substances and behaviors, they developed what they called the Transtheoretical Model of Change, or TTM.

TTM is an integrative approach that describes key components of behavior change and includes ideas about stages of change, processes of change, markers of change, and contexts of change. We'll chat about this model just enough to give you an impressionistic sense of what, in their view, are the components of change. Your work isn't learning their model but tackling our questions and exercises at the end of this discus-sion and effecting real change in your life.

Their approach has been shown to apply to three types of behavior change: initially establishing patterns of behavior, modifying habitual patterns of behavior, and stopping addictive patterns of use. DiClemente explains: "While the factors that lead a particular individual into addic-tion and out of it are unique to that individual, the process of becoming addicted and of recovery follow a common path. The path is also com-mon across individuals and across addictive behaviors." Recovery pro-grams work for exactly this reason, because most people get addicted in the same way and recover in the same way. Their model presents five stages of change.

1. Precontemplation

In precontemplation you don't believe that you have a problem, even if others think you do, and you have no intention of changing or stopping the addictive behavior in the foreseeable future. You are not yet contem-plating any change. If you have addictive problems and are reading this book, this probably isn't you!—you've probably passed through precon-templation at least as far as the contemplation phase of change.

2. Contemplation

In the contemplation stage, you believe that you *do* have a problem and are considering doing something about it in the foreseeable future—just not right now. You are contemplating change but aren't taking any concrete actions that support change or amount to change. Change is on your radar screen, but that's about it.

3. Preparation

In the preparation stage you acknowledge that you have a problem, believe that you can do something about it, and start setting the stage for change. Talking to your friends about the problem and cutting down on your substance use fall into this category. In this stage, you do some things in support of change but not in a way that amounts to a complete change of direction or a complete course of action. This is like finally buying those expensive pastels and trying them out on cheap paper just to see what they look like but not taking the plunge and making art with them.

4. Action

In the action stage you engage in an array of new behaviors, including the most important ones, such as becoming abstinent from the addictive behavior, and you begin to make other significant life changes that support continued abstinence, such as regularly attending twelve-step meetings, changing your circles of friends, and so on. You likely experience some setbacks and also learn from those setbacks and by becoming more mindful and watchful, tend not to repeat those same mistakes.

5. Maintenance

In the maintenance stage, your new recovery behavior stabilizes over time (stabilizing for at least six months meets the definition of "maintenance") and becomes integrated into other areas of your life. In the same way that physicians describe cancer survivors, clinicians refer to abstinent addicts as being in remission from the addiction. You are still addicted, but you are not now acting on your addiction.

The Process of Change

A person's movement through the stages of change has often been described in terms of spiral action. More often than not, people recycle back into a previous stage at some point, sometimes briefly and sometimes indefinitely. When the return to addictive behavior is an isolated incident, clinicians refer to it as a lapse. When a person continues to use and finds himself or herself back in the precontemplation stage or the contemplation stage of recovery, that's considered a full-blown relapse.

That this spiral change happens so often that it is a hallmark feature of the process should alert you to the possibility that your recovery will not look like a straight line—and that if it doesn't, that's nothing to feel ashamed of or embarrassed about. The goal is always to start again and not to bad-mouth your efforts. In this context, starting again means moving one stage forward in the direction of preparation, action, and maintenance.

The model also describes certain processes of change that are required if change is to happen. The first five (discussed below) pertain to how people think and feel about their situation and are especially important in the early stages of change. The last six involve behavioral actions and are crucial to the later stages of change. These are exactly like steps familiar to you from the creative process: how actually writing your novel is different from imagining that you want to write a novel, how changing aspects of your environment (such as moving to a quieter room in the house) positively affects your ability to write your novel, and so on.

As you explore these eleven processes, you might want to consider how each one applies to your current situation. Is it, for example, time to increase your awareness of your actual alcohol use, time to recognize how your drinking is negatively affecting both your writing and your relationships, time to let go of the myth that you need your scotch in order to be creative, and so on? Give each of the following some real thought.

Cognitive and Behavioral Processes

The first process of change is raising your consciousness, increasing your awareness, and recognizing that a problem exists. You do this by acknowledging the negative consequences of your addictive behaviors and surrendering to the truth that you have been out of control for some time with respect to these addictive behaviors.

The second process is engaging your feelings about your addictive behaviors, feelings that you can then use to help you enter active recovery. When you engage your feelings and recognize that you are genuinely saddened by the way you're living a chaotic, unfulfilling life—or by the way you're not getting your creative work done—that depth of emotion can open the door to real change.

The third process is engaging in a thorough self-evaluation where you bring to mind your cherished values, your important needs, your strong beliefs, and your highest aspirations and then carefully examine how your addictive behaviors negatively affect you in each of these areas. The first two steps, increasing your awareness and engaging your feelings, allow for this third step, a thoroughgoing examination of how your life plan is being sabotaged by your addictive behaviors.

The fourth process is examining the consequences of your addictive behaviors on your environment: how your behaviors are negatively affecting those you love, your professional relationships (for instance, with your literary agent, the owners of the galleries at which you show, or your boss at your day job), and your physical environment (for instance, the disorganization of your painting studio). Examining these particular negative consequences furthers your thorough analysis of how your addiction is not serving you.

The fifth process is recognizing how cultural myths, conventions, and institutions—for instance, our culture-wide association of fine wines and champagne with romance, the popularity of betting pools in offices, the use of gambling in the form of lotteries to fund schools, and so on —play into your addictive tendencies.

The sixth process is taking responsibility for your thoughts and actions, making more conscious and mindful choices, committing to new thoughts (for instance, to the thought that your addiction really does not serve you or your creative life) and new behaviors (for instance, no longer frequenting bars), and moving steadfastly in the direction of real change.

The seventh process is conditioning yourself to respond differently to cues (for instance, conditioning yourself to have a cup of tea rather than a scotch to celebrate the end of your daily writing stint), establishing new associations between signals to use and your behavior (for example, no longer taking the end of the run of a play as a cue to go on a drinking binge), and substituting recovery behaviors for addictive behaviors in response to conditioned triggers to use (for instance, substituting a Narcotics Anonymous meeting for a joint in response to feeling down about the progress of your current novel).

The eighth process is beginning to avoid stimuli that trigger the addictive behavior, for instance avoiding partying with band members, avoiding porn sites, or avoiding that junket to Las Vegas, and beginning to create stimuli that encourage recovery behaviors, for instance, by putting up affirmations in your painting studio or by recording a relaxation tape that you play when you start to grow anxious.

The ninth process is taking the recovery behaviors you've established in one setting and employing them in other settings where you customarily use. For instance, if you've learned certain deep-breathing techniques that work to calm you but so far have employed them only as part of your morning centering practice, now you want to take that behavior into the field and begin to use it at your stressful day job or in the painting studio.

The tenth process is establishing rewards for recovery behaviors. This could mean buying that expensive watercolor paper as a reward for a significant stretch of sobriety or celebrating writing without using by taking a stroll at the beach. This process is also about eliminating rewards related to your addictive behaviors, for example, by saving for a piece of jewelry rather than by associating such self-gifts with gambling winnings.

The eleventh process is creating a support system of people who encourage your sobriety. This includes family members and friends, whom you clearly apprise of your recovery intentions; helping professionals such as therapists, coaches, and addictions specialists; individuals who agree to be there for you when you ask for their help (and who comprise your safe list of phone contacts); and the peer support provided at self-help meetings.

The idea of stages of change is a simple, useful one that, because of its simplicity, has been employed in a wide variety of settings—among them weight-loss programs, injury-prevention programs, and alcohol and drug treatment programs—to help people understand where they are and what steps they need to take to move in the desired direction. It has been used, for example, in community-based HIV-positive treatment programs to help at-risk individuals move toward increased condom carrying and increased condom use; facilitators in these programs design interventions that attempt to move each participant at least one stage of change forward.

We think that you can see how this model might meet you where you currently are. It would be lovely if you could leap from "I have no problem" to full recovery, but it has been repeatedly shown that the more effective strategy is to help you move mindfully and consciously one stage at a time in the right direction: from precontemplation to real contemplation to actual preparation to substantial action to thoughtful maintenance. You may be someone who goes, by virtue of an amazing transition, from complete denial to full recovery, but the likelihood is far greater that your path will be the typical one of stage-by-stage change and growth.

CREATIVE-RECOVERY JOURNAL QUESTIONS

1. In what change stage are you with respect to your addictive problems? You may well be in different stages with respect to different problems: for instance, in the action stage with respect to your drinking but only in precontemplation with respect to your sex addiction or your eating disorder. Think about each of your addiction issues separately—including those where you think you have no problem whatsoever.

2. What, in your estimation, is the essential difference between moving toward change and actually changing? What are some markers of movement toward change? What are some markers of actual change?
3. How can you use your creative nature to move you one stage in the right direction toward recovery? Try to describe the many ways that your creative nature could be employed to help you move from precontemplation to contemplation, from contemplation to action, and so on.

Moving Toward Change

It may be difficult to imagine what it looks like to move through the stages of change. Here are two examples that illustrate the mental and physical ways we can make change happen.

Starting to Run: Susan's Story

When I was in my teens and early twenties, I carried around an extra twenty pounds. Having been a highly active, thin child, I did not identify with this chubby teen version of myself and I felt self-conscious and discouraged about it for years. Well into my twenties, I'd get fed up with myself, go on crazy diets based on extreme deprivation that I could not sustain, fail as the weight returned, and feel helpless and hopeless. I bounced between strategies of overcontrol and undercontrol, neither of which was effective.

Occasionally this dynamic would include diet-doctor shots or diet pills. Looking back at it now, I have empathy for that younger version of myself as someone who lost her mother at age eight and her father by age fifteen, learned to minimize many real feelings as an adult child of an alcoholic, fell into a sedentary behavior pattern when living in a new environment with relatives, and turned to food for comfort. I can still recall the mixture of feelings I had when I sat around and watched television weight-loss ads and fitness-center ads. A hazy combination of guilt for not doing something and despair about past failures would alternate with a dim hope and a belief that real change could be achieved.

Despite the promise of these ads, and despite my intellectual understanding about eating less and exercising more, I had no clear idea how to do it. Nor was I seeking the necessary emotional or practical support I needed for change. Indeed, how could I when I had no clue that I needed any such support? I was drifting back and forth between the precontemplation, contemplation, and preparation stages of change until, in my late twenties, I finally succeeded in stepping out of the vicious circle I was in with my weight.

A number of variables came together to move me in the right direction and support enduring change. I was maturing, developing a more authentic relationship with my emotions, feeling less deprived financially, starting my career, and participating in a loving relationship. I was also fortunate to have a good friend and colleague who was a dedicated runner and who found herself participating in an ongoing University of California–San Francisco health study on exercise. Observing her good behaviors for a year (yes, preparing takes that long sometimes!), I complained to her about my weight, and she told me what I could do; and I was ready to do it. She took me to buy a pair of running shoes. Being a style hound, I bribed myself by buying an outfit to run in. I started running.

At first I ran around the block for ten minutes, feeling pathetic and hoping no one would see me. In time I built up the distance, the pace, and the frequency until I was running for thirty minutes four days a week. My friend helped me move from the contemplation stage through the preparation stage to the action stage of change. That was 1978, and I'm still running, moderately but consistently. I maintain a healthy weight that I feel good about. Probably you, too, have contemplated some sensible change and have even made regular preparations. I hope that you will move into the action phase soon—maybe as soon as by the end of this chapter!

The Case of Richard

Richard P., a talented portrait photographer, arrived at the chemical-dependency program with the following story. Twelve years earlier, after a significant drinking career of twenty years, he had started experiencing withdrawal symptoms when he tried to take his customary brief vacation from drinking to dry out. He ended up in a hospital emergency department with withdrawal delirium, or the DTs. In his hospital room he began seeing frightening creatures, an experience that scared him out of the contemplation stage of change. Over the next several years, he moved from preparation and action into maintenance.

During the maintenance phase, Richard spent half of his sober years doing what his addiction counselors suggested. He went to chemical-dependency treatment and was in recovery groups; he attended Alcoholics Anonymous meetings regularly; he got an AA sponsor and worked the steps. Richard started out as a counselor's dream: he did what he was told and did it without resentment. He remained sober and seemed to be progressing in all areas of his life.

He was single and he sometimes dated. He had friends, many of whom attended the same AA meetings he did. His nonaddicted photographer colleagues were happy to meet him at a coffee shop instead of at a bar. He mended many emotional fences with his brother and other family members as he worked the twelve steps of AA. He had managed to keep his day job during his drinking days; his longtime employer, worried about Richard's occasional unexplained absences when he was drinking, was actually relieved when Richard admitted his alcohol problem and sought help. His boss valued Richard's work, liked him when he was sober, and retained him as an employee at the photography studio.

What happened to cause the relapse? After about six years of sobriety and good recovery behavior, Richard's close-knit circle of friends at AA meetings started to disband. First his sponsor moved out of the area and he and Richard slowly lost contact. Several of his AA buddies subsequently drifted away and never got replaced with new connections. Richard did not seek out a new sponsor, figuring that he was able to stay sober on his own after six years. Over time, Richard stopped going to meetings, stopped reaching out to others, and stopped engaging in a regular practice of recovery.

People thought that Richard was doing fine, and so did Richard. Granted, he'd become increasingly isolated, but he didn't seem to let that bother him. Then he woke up one Saturday morning with a painful toothache. When he called his dentist's office, he was dismayed to hear that he could not be seen until Monday morning. He was legitimately suffering, and his decisional balance started to shift in the service of drinking for relief.

He weighed the pros and cons and decided that it would be all right to buy some Jim Beam for pain relief until Monday morning. He felt confident that he could control his use after twelve years of sobriety. In fact, he drank only moderately that weekend. He had two drinks on Saturday night and two more on Sunday night. He did not experience the loss of control that characterized his drinking in the past. He went to the dentist on Monday morning, had his tooth fixed, and experienced relief.

A few months later Richard decided that it would be safe for him to drink beer while watching football on TV on Sundays. After all, he rationalized to himself, he had not lost control when he drank hard liquor to numb his dental pain, and he deserved to relax and have some fun. He began drinking a couple of beers every Sunday, alone in his apartment, his beers keeping him company. Over the next six months, those couple of beers morphed into a six-pack every Friday, Saturday, and Sunday night.

One weekend while Richard was drinking, he decided to hop in the company car and pick up another six-pack. He made a wrong move and ended up getting into an accident. The company car was noticeably damaged, but no one was injured. The police arrived, issued him a DUI, and invited him to spend the night in jail. In addition to having to pay the fines and lawyer fees associated with his relapse, Richard was fired by his employer, a year short of his eligibility for retirement. The party was over.

Richard was fifty when he got sober the first time, sixty-two when he relapsed, and sixty-three years old when he regained his sobriety. He jumpstarted his recovery momentum by returning to a chemical-dependency program, went back to regular AA meetings, got a new sponsor, and started reworking the twelve steps. He learned some important things about the pitfalls of discontinuing his recovery practice, about isolation, and about the process of relapse. He had progressed through the stages of change to get sober the first time, had fallen back through the rabbit hole into active addiction, and had found his way back from addiction into recovery. This is a not an atypical pattern.

Why Change?

In these first four chapters we've asked you to look at your risks for addiction, to locate your place along the abuse continuum, and to assess your readiness to change. We can't know if you are a late-stage alcoholic musician or a young writer or painter worried about some troubling addictive tendencies. What we presume is that you are concerned enough about your addictive nature to have gravitated to this book, which almost certainly means that there are some profitable changes you might make in your life.

We have the hunch that you know that you have some changes to make. Maybe you understand that you are at risk for an addiction and want to take precautionary, prophylactic measures. Maybe your use or your behaviors worry you and you want to nip your potential addiction in the bud. Maybe you are a full-fledged addict, know it, and know that you need to change right now. We think you have at least an inkling that change in the direction of recovery would serve you.

Right now you may be anywhere in the change cycle, in precontemplation with respect to your alcohol use, in contemplation with respect to your gambling, in maintenance with respect to your overeating. How can you know where you are? We think that the best way may be for you to simply write down any thoughts that have arisen as you've read along. That is one of the simple (but not necessarily easy) exercises that we leave you with at the end of this chapter.

Creative Exercises

We hope you have already warmed up for this chapter's creative exercises by making some notes to yourself about the change process in your creative-recovery journal. Building upon what you've already learned about your risk factors for addiction and your place on the abuse continuum, we want you to use your creativity now to identify your current stage of change. Once again we encourage you to experiment with all the exercises, not just the ones that are easiest for you.

1. For the writer in you

Write a poem, short story, or play in which your main character gradually changes. Describe the character's setting and motivation. What precipitated the change? What happens after the change? Notice your own responses to your character. Did your character's change influence how you feel toward him or her? How so? What does your character have to teach you about your own stage of change?

2. For the visual artist in you

Draw symbolic representations of yourself at different stages of your relationship to the substance or behavior that is giving you the most trouble. What would contemplation look like compared with action? Which stage of change best represents your current position? If you struggle with cross-addiction (for example, with sexual compulsions in addition to chemical dependency), repeat the exercise, drawing the other addictive behavior this time. Do the drawings look similar or different? How so? Take note of what you're thinking and feeling while doing this exercise.

3. For the dancer in you

Pick an addiction that does not apply to you. In your mind's eye, get into the skin and body of a person who is addicted that way. How would you use movement to represent that person differently at each stage of change along the path to recovery? What sort of music would you choose to accompany your dance for the different stages? What do these dances tell you about your own stage of change?

Now repeat the exercise choosing the substance or risky behavior that you *do* struggle with, again representing the various stages of change.

What stage of change are you currently in? What do you notice about applying this to yourself rather than to someone else?

4. For the scientist in you

Are these stages of change more behavioral markers or psychological markers? What is your analysis? Identify your own current stage of change. Which markers did you use to self-assess? How do you feel about your results?

5. For the dreamer in you

Picture yourself really changed. Are you more the same person or more a different person? Imagine yourself keeping the best aspects of your former self as you embrace the most satisfying aspects of your newly changed self. What aspects of your old self do you want to keep? What aspects do you want to add and cultivate in your recovery? What will you need to help you do that?

Postscript

We hope you are now equipped with a better sense of your risk factors for addiction, your current place on the abuse continuum, and your stage of change. As you consider what you want to do next about all of this, it is time to acknowledge your addiction challenges.

5 🔺 *Your Addiction Challenges*

So far we've presented information on the look of addiction and invited you to begin thinking about whether, and to what extent, you might be at risk—or worse, already in the throes of an addiction. Now we want to explain how you can move from not quite acknowledging your addiction challenges to fully acknowledging them and entering recovery.

Avoiding Acknowledgment

There are various predictable ways that alcoholics and addicts tend to deny their addiction problems. For instance, you might mistakenly attribute the negative consequences of your use to something other than the substance or addictive behavior: you might blame your husband for being "overly sensitive about alcohol" because he had an alcoholic mother, or you might justify acting out sexually because you're stressed.

You might allow others to enable your continued use and secretly appreciate their misguided efforts to protect you from the natural consequences of your addictive behavior. Or you might compare yourself to stereotypical alcoholics or addicts whose disease is more progressed than yours and use their fallen state as evidence that you don't have a problem. You might do this by, for example, thinking, "I don't drink as much as Joe; he's the real alcoholic" or "I can still paint, I can't be an addict."

This is the sort of tricky creature that we are, happy in our bondage and defended against understanding the truth of our situation. To keep from changing, you might collapse into surplus powerlessness and argue that because changing behavior is difficult, it is impossible, contriving to make the situation seem hopeless. Here you are feeling sorry for yourself and finding ways of rationalizing your desire not to change anything. The more you typically say to yourself "This is too hard" or "This is impossible" with respect to behavior change, the more you prevent yourself from moving from the precontemplation phase of change to the contemplation phase or from the contemplation phase to preparation to action.

Similarly, you may employ rigid personal requirements in order to avoid change, maybe telling yourself "I don't do groups" or "I can't stand the discomfort without drugs," where "don't" and "can't" in those sentences just mean "won't." It is hard for us to believe that we are as defensive and in denial as this, but most people are, even those without a full-blown addiction. Just think of how many creative people are avoiding noticing that they haven't worked on their novel for a month or that their acting career is stalled. Not wanting to notice is the usual way.

In her autobiographical account of her recovery from alcoholism, the writer and columnist Caroline Knapp offered the following description of her process of moving past denial into acknowledgment: "As I sat in Michael's kitchen that morning, reading *Esquire* and feeling so paralyzed, I remembered my father's words about 'insight' almost always being a 'rearrangement of fact.' Fact One: I drank too much. Fact Two: I was desperately unhappy. I had always thought: *I drink because I'm unhappy.* Just then I shifted the equation, rearranged the words: *Maybe, just maybe,*

I'm unhappy because I drink. This was not a hopeful sensation, a moment of optimism. I felt desperate, and all I had to cling to for that instant was a mere seed of faith: *maybe* things would change if I quit drinking; *maybe* drinking was in fact the problem and not the solution. I saw my sister that afternoon and asked her to find me a rehab program. Two months later, on February 19, I had my last drink."

In order to acknowledge a problem like your addictive tendencies, you must increase your awareness; engage your feelings about the effects of your addictive behavior; and begin to recognize how the addictive behavior negatively affects your life, your values, and the people you care about. This is hard to do when you begin to lose control and can't stop using your substance or engaging in your behavior, as it is frightening and humiliating to admit that you are out of control. So you deny the presence of a problem. You aren't just trying to deny that you drink too much or that you've become obese: you are trying to deny what you perceive as your humiliating weakness and failure.

The author and addiction specialist Stephanie Brown explains: "The turn towards alcohol leads to a point at which the individual ceases to choose alcohol freely. The need for alcohol becomes the central focus (most often unconscious and therefore denied) and, in effect, the organizer of the individual's behavior and thinking. The need to include more and more alcohol in one's life without disturbing the central belief in self-control becomes the dominant focus of daily life." You can see how hard it is to acknowledge a problem when you have organized your life around a set of false beliefs: that you are in complete control (when you are not) and that you have no problem (when you do). When you secretly believe that you need the substance or behavior and that giving it up would prove too great a sacrifice (and maybe an impossibility), you minimize the impact the addiction is having on your life or completely deny that a problem exists.

Challenging this denial by connecting the dots between the addictive behavior and the consequences of the addictive behavior is the central goal for therapists working with active alcoholics and addicts at this early stage. Movement out of the addictive stage into the transition stage toward recovery represents the breaking down of this denial and distortion and acceptance by the addict of the need for abstinence. Before, drinking or snorting cocaine was seen as the need; now abstinence is seen as the need. This fundamental shift is a crucial part of the transition process and the fundamental shift that you, too, will want to make if you suspect (as you peek through your denial) that you have addiction problems. You want to move from seeing your addiction as the need to seeing abstinence as the need.

Acknowledging the Problem

The main way to acknowledge the problem is to break free from the delusion of your addiction and to realize that you are an addict and that you need to start the path to recovery. We hope that the exercises and journal questions have been helping you to understand your addiction through clear eyes—free from self-delusion. The key to this work is full disclosure. It is now time to tell yourself everything: the scary, the embarrassing, the painful, and the sordid.

You might want to try out the following exercise to help be truthful with yourself. Dr. William Miller and his colleagues at the University of New Mexico, feeling that addicted clients in the early stages of change were not being met by their service providers, developed an approach they called motivational enhancement. Using a technique they call motivational interviewing, this approach focuses on meeting clients where they are rather than trying to force them into some later stage of change. You can use this interviewing approach with yourself, meeting yourself wherever you happen to be on the abuse continuum and in whatever stage of change you find yourself.

Miller describes motivational interviewing as "a person-centered, goal-oriented approach for facilitating change through exploring and resolving ambivalence." Ambivalence is viewed as a "fluctuating state of readiness or willingness to change that can be influenced by situational factors and certain types of interpersonal interactions." The goals of the therapist using this technique are to stay empathic and nonjudgmental toward the client's stated position; maintain a curious, caring, and interested stance while helping clients safely explore their honest ambivalence; avoid arguments, power struggles, and an authoritarian, controlling attitude; and stay with the client's actual stage of change instead of jumping ahead without him or her.

Miller provides therapists with the following ABCDEFGH mnemonic that they can use with their clients. We now ask you to interview yourself using this same device. Try on the role of therapist as you ask yourself questions and work toward acknowledging your addiction problems. Think through how you can serve as exactly this sort of interviewer for yourself, someone who cares, who's curious, and who can help you explore your honest ambivalence about both wanting to stop and wanting to use.

Give ADVICE. Provide yourself with simple, well-timed information. This means educating yourself on the short-term and long-term effects of alcohol, if alcohol is your drug of choice, on the difference between a healthy sex life and a sex addiction, if sex is your drug of choice, and so on.

Remove BARRIERS. Try to help yourself problem solve and overcome practical or psychological barriers to change. Knock down your defensive walls with the same energy and muscle power that you would use to demolish an actual wall.

Provide CHOICES. Clarify the kinds of choices that are available to you and make clear choices that favor sobriety. Begin by thinking through ways you might live your life, including your creative life, that would support recovery.

Decrease DESIRABILITY. Stop making your use seem like a good, charming, or desirable thing. Focus on the negative effects of using and call yourself on any inconsistencies and distortions you employ to underestimate your difficulties.

Practice EMPATHY. Really listen to yourself, accurately reflect back your thoughts, maintain a supportive stance throughout this interview process, and pay genuine respect to your efforts to change.

Provide FEEDBACK. Give yourself relevant, accurate feedback about your situation and make use of this process to keep yourself posted about the current state of your addiction and about your recovery efforts.

Clarify GOALS. Clarify goals for yourself that are realistic, desirable, and attainable and try to determine what you are really aiming for in life. For each goal, clarify the details of the plan that you will put in place to achieve the goal.

Actively HELP. Help yourself to honestly examine your situation and stay genuinely involved and supportive, not just for a day or a week but over the long haul. Be a help to yourself, not a hindrance—both in this interview process and, more important, in life.

CREATIVE-RECOVERY EXERCISES

1. Instead of using the mnemonic system above, interview yourself for your favorite TV or magazine. Pretend to interview with *Spin* magazine about your music, then open up to discuss your drinking habits. You might want to use a pad and pen and act like a cub reporter on assignment, or you might want to put two chairs face-to-face and move from chair to chair as you ask and answer the questions you pose.

   Start simply with a question such as, "So, you've been thinking that maybe you have some problems with your drinking?" Then answer it. Then patiently ask yourself the next natural question, then the next, staying with the process for as long as you can—and until you feel that you have genuinely dealt with your ambivalence and have acknowledged any problems that you were previously denying.

2. You may think that there are ways that your addiction serves your creativity. We would like you to talk yourself out of that false belief right now. Spend as much time as it takes convincing yourself that your addiction does not serve your creativity. If you can't manage to convince yourself, at least do an honorable job of presenting yourself with evidence of your addiction's destructive side and with good arguments for recovery.

   If you want to take a dramatic shortcut and skip the conversation, just announce out loud "My addiction is no good for my creating!" and repeat that warning, admonition, or battle cry many times a day, sometimes at the top of your lungs. The best way to convince yourself is to patiently point out the negatives

---

of your use: how little creating you actually get done because you are so busy distracting yourself with your addiction, how the work you've always dreamed of doing is eluding you because of the haze in which you live, how you keep your life (and your creative life) in complete chaos by chasing highs. Focus on the negatives of your use now and try to convince yourself that your addiction is a genuine problem.

3. Acknowledging that you have a problem with an addiction has both a thinking component and a feeling component, describe in your own words the difference between thinking about your problem and engaging your feelings about your problem. Have you ever actually engaged your feelings with regard to your addiction problems?

You can tell that we are asking you to use all of your creative talents, including your penchant for whimsy and play, in this exercise. It is a whimsical idea to ask you to step outside yourself and interview yourself about problems that you actually don't want to acknowledge. But what is magical and wonderful, and a testament to the resilience of the species and the power of your creative nature, is that you can in fact do just this. You can interview yourself about your drinking, even though you don't want to know about your drinking; you can interview yourself about your gambling, even though you don't want to know about your gambling. This is possible because part of you wants to save yourself: you are enlisting that part in the service of helping you acknowledge your embarrassing problems.

When you have finished interviewing yourself, consider the possibility of repeating this process with another human being who is knowledgeable about addiction and recovery and having him or her interview you in the same way. For some of you, that person may be a family member, a friend, or a fellow traveler in recovery. For others that person will be a mental health professional.

In the following two case studies, you will meet a software designer who was able to acknowledge his alcohol problem early on, to his great benefit, and a modern dancer who was not yet able to acknowledge the depths of her bulimia and methamphetamine addiction, losing herself in the process.

The Case of Cliff

Cliff L. was a successful African American software designer in his forties who came to Susan for help with stress, anxiety, and relationship issues and discovered that his drinking was a primary problem. He'd had a few panic attacks some months before after an exhausting push at work that interfered with his time with his girlfriend. He clearly needed to improve his self-care and learn to relax more effectively.

Susan and Cliff soon came to see that his increased anxiety was centrally related to long-standing fears about fully committing himself in a love relationship. In the past he had sabotaged relationships as the emotional intimacy deepened, and he did not want to repeat that pattern with his current girlfriend, who, as it happened, was Caucasian.

During the course of therapy, Cliff got engaged and planned to marry his girlfriend. He reported drinking a couple of beers or glasses of wine a few times a week without any particular problems. He mentioned past drinking experiences of "getting hammered" on a few occasions but minimized and rationalized the circumstances, and at first his drinking stayed under the radar in therapy.

On three occasions over the course of the first year of his therapy Cliff sheepishly admitted that he had experienced binge-drinking episodes. He would start out with his customary couple of beers and end up drinking about ten drinks during the evening. After one of these binge episodes, Cliff was told that he had made racist comments about his future wife's conservative white family. Cliff was mortified, as he was a progressive liberal who prided himself on his egalitarian outlook. More to the point, he was terrified that his fiancée would find out about his comments, not trust him or love him anymore, and end the engagement.

As a result of this incident, Cliff acknowledged the problem that his drinking posed and decided that he would stop drinking completely. He did just that. He got more honest with himself about the stress he felt as a black male dealing with his fiancée's Caucasian family, interactions that often left him feeling marginalized and devalued. He started to talk more openly with his fiancée about the pressure he felt, which provided her with more room to share her own ambivalent feelings with him. Their intimacy deepened, and they married soon thereafter. She never learned about his bad behavior while drunk, and eventually he forgave himself, too. Cliff was relatively quick to acknowledge his problem, and that made all the difference in the world. Because of this early acknowledgment, he experienced what in recovery circles is called a high bottom, suffering only minimal negative consequences from his alcohol use.

The Case of Kelly

Kelly M., an attractive thirty-four-year-old divorced dancer, was referred to Susan for outpatient psychotherapy after being discharged from a university hospital where she'd been treated medically for an esophageal tear related to chronic binging and purging. In addition to her five-year history of bulimia, Kelly also confessed to an amphetamine-abuse problem related to her desire to control her weight. Although she had refused many prior treatment recommendations, Kelly was scared enough this time by her medical consequences to stop the methamphetamine use and agree to enter weekly therapy, although she remained reluctant to go to Narcotics Anonymous—a sign that she was not yet really acknowledging her problems.

Kelly had a pattern of alternating severe dieting and amphetamine use with periods of binge eating and purging. Although she initially portrayed herself as actively involved in her local modern-dance community, she eventually admitted that she'd pretty much stopped dancing as her use of speed increased. Her elaborate plans to return to dancing never materialized.

The therapy initially focused on disrupting the diet-drug–binge-purge pattern by normalizing her eating habits; that is, by working toward her eating and keeping down three meals a day, with adequate calories, and eating a wide range of foods. At first she kept her weekly therapy appointments. As she ate more adequately, she was able to decrease the frequency of her binge-eating and purging episodes. She continued to worry about her weight, but as her weight gain was minimal, she was able, for the most part, to stay away from the amphetamines. Without minimizing Kelly's drug use as a continuing problem, Susan began to discuss other aspects of her emotional life and relationships with her.

After a six-month period of reasonable progress, Kelly became involved with an old boyfriend with whom she had previously used drugs. She denied getting back into the amphetamine use, but Susan expressed concern, more so when Kelly began missing sessions. After about two months of canceling and rescheduling therapy sessions, she stopped showing up and did not return Susan's calls. When she turned up again eight months later, she was a self-described mess. She had returned to the unhealthy dieting, speed use, and vicious cycle of binging and purging.

Kelly had lost a lot of ground, and Susan strongly encouraged her to accept a referral to a more intensive level of care for the eating disorder and the drug abuse. Continuing not to acknowledge the seriousness of her situation, she explained that she had really just come in to say good-bye. She was moving to Las Vegas, where her boyfriend had arranged for her to have breast augmentation surgery and to get a job in a strip club as a lap dancer (as her modern-dance aspirations had been completely discarded by this time). Susan maintained the hope that Kelly would enter recovery at a later point in her life, as no story is over until it's over, but Kelly's refusal to acknowledge her problems, and the negative consequences of that refusal, remained hallmarks of their time together.

CREATIVE-RECOVERY JOURNAL QUESTIONS

1. What barriers do you erect to keep yourself from acknowledging the problems you have with addiction?
2. What would it look like to rearrange your belief system in the direction of honestly acknowledging the harm that your addictive tendencies are causing you?
3. What do you want to do about the fact that you can sometimes see yourself clearly and sometimes not see yourself at all? When are you most able to see yourself clearly?
4. Do you have a problem with some substance or behavior? If so,

> are you ready to acknowledge that problem? *How* will you acknowledge it?

Using Self-Help Groups

Self-help groups not only serve you in ongoing recovery: they help you right at the start when you are beginning to acknowledge your problem. As you sit and listen to an alcoholic admit to being an alcoholic and describe the tricks she used to play to maintain her drinking, you are pushed in the direction of noticing the tricks that you, too, have played: you see yourself in these reports and portrayals, your denial is dented, and you come closer to admitting the truth of your situation.

The efficacy of group support in the recovery process is a well-established principle and one that is at the heart of most formal treatment programs around the world. In addition to attending group therapy facilitated by mental health practitioners in treatment centers, recovering clients are usually encouraged to develop relationships in their own communities that support sobriety. These self-help groups are also the place where you are likely to genuinely acknowledge your problem for the first time, as you listen to the stories of others and, at some point, stand up and share your story.

Since addiction is considered a lifestyle-related chronic problem, people continue to benefit from support at all stages of the process. This is true whether you became sober on your own, without a formal structure, or went to an inpatient or outpatient treatment program. In addition to the potentially supportive role of friends and family, an accessible way to develop ongoing support is through established self-help groups such as twelve-step programs (for example, Alcoholics Anonymous, Sex Addicts

Anonymous, Gamblers Anonymous, Marijuana Anonymous, Narcotics Anonymous, and so forth) and alternatives such as LifeRing Secular Recovery and Women for Sobriety.

Many of you are familiar with self-help groups, and if you are, you may already have developed a strong opinion, either pro or con, about a specific program. Indeed, you may have bounced in and out of such groups over the years with various degrees of success. Even if you have strong negative opinions about self-help groups and even if you have tried them and found them lacking, we ask you to give them another try. If you are basing your aversion on stereotypes, treat them as just that, stereotypes, and let those stereotypes go. If you are basing your aversion on your experience of meetings, remember that meetings within a given program can differ significantly in the quality of recovery present, so you might not have found the right meeting and may have given up too soon. In either case, give a meeting a try.

You may have avoided self-help groups because you fear embarrassment, hate the idea of looking weak or sick, or anticipate that a stigma will attach to you if you identify yourself as in need of help. We want you to look at this with new eyes, eyes that are open to the possibility that an established self-help group may be of real use to you. Think of it this way: dancers benefit from dance companies, actors benefit from repertory companies, and people struggling with addictive tendencies also benefit from the kind of support that only a group with common interests and common goals can afford.

Step 1 of the Alcoholics Anonymous program directly addresses the task of acknowledging the problem of addiction by stating: "We admitted we were powerless over alcohol—that our lives had become unmanageable." Of course, many people, even those who admit to a problem, do not feel that their lives have become unmanageable. If that is your response, start by admitting what *has* in fact become unmanageable about your use. The level of unmanageability is often directly related to how progressed the addiction has become. If, for example, your relationships have been affected by your addiction, but not your job, legal status, or health, consider yourself lucky that you are acknowledging the problem at a relatively early stage, before the addiction has affected all areas of your life.

Various alternatives to the twelve-step programs have developed over the years, usually as a reaction to the twelve-step emphasis on spirituality and related ideas of individual dependency, loss of control, and powerlessness. One of the earlier self-help alternatives, Rational Recovery (RR), was created by a social worker named Jack Trimpey and emphasized self-reliance and self-control, using strategies from cognitive-behavioral therapy. RR taught recovering individuals to "exert direct control over their emotions, moods, and actions, including their drinking and their drug use." RR agreed with AA about the importance of abstinence but championed the idea of personal responsibility and eschewed ideas of powerlessness as "deadly."

More recently, LifeRing Secular Recovery (LSR) has become the primary secular alternative to the twelve-step programs. With roots in an earlier organization, Secular Organizations for Sobriety, the LSR philosophy is summarized in three words: Sobriety, Secularity, and Self-Help. Meetings emphasize interpersonal connection and sober people "working side by side as members of one family." LifeRing emphasizes strengthening the feedback loop between the sober voice in each of its members, what it calls the S-to-S connection, and weakening the loop between the addict voice in each member, the A-to-A connection. S-to-S interactions support sobriety and recovery; A-to-A interactions support addiction.

With respect to acknowledging the problem, LSR emphasizes the idea of a cognitive shift in the direction of honesty and self-awareness and the necessity for what it calls the Sobriety Priority.

Another self-help option is Women for Sobriety (WFS). Founded in 1975 by Jean Kirkpatrick, WFS is described as the first national self-help program for women alcoholics. WFS promotes a thirteen-statement program of "positivity that encourages emotional and spiritual growth" called the "New Life" Acceptance Program. Acknowledging the problem of addiction happens in Level 1, where you accept alcoholism as a physical disorder and make the following announcement: "I have a life-threatening problem that once had me. *I now take charge of my life. I accept the responsibility.*"

For a time Artists Anonymous groups flourished in various locales, making use of basic twelve-step ideas to help participants promote sobriety and increase creativity. Chapters of Artists Anonymous still come and go, and you may want to check to see if such a group is functioning in your community. Big cities with substantial numbers of arts professionals in recovery, such as New York, Nashville, and Los Angeles, are most likely to have twelve-step meetings attended regularly by artists and musicians, who choose among meetings via word of mouth. Asking around in your own locale remains your best bet in finding such meetings.

Musicians and other music professionals may get additional help in locating such resources by calling the National Academy of Recording Arts and Sciences (NARAS) MusiCares Musicians' Assistance Program in Los Angeles (see the resources section). While certain inpatient treatment centers focus on working with an artist clientele (see resources), and despite the occasional appearance of an Artists Anonymous group, there does not look to be a viable national self-help support network for creative people at this time, so your best bet is to make use of traditional programs like AA, LSR, or WFS. In addition, you might think about getting some of your fellow artists-in-recovery together and begin an artists' recovery support group in your locale.

Each of these various programs is designed to help you acknowledge your addiction problems. As a creative person who not only highly prizes individuality but also organizes your life around the principle of individual effort, you are likely to have an extra antipathy to self-help groups and to the idea of group work. You recognize that no great novel could ever be written by a committee and extrapolate from that truth about the lack of creativity present in groups to the idea that all group work is suspect and even contemptible. But that isn't true. Groups can and do serve a real function in the recovery process—at the beginning of that process, as you work to acknowledge your problem, and throughout the process, with its many problematic ins and outs and ups and downs.

CREATIVE-RECOVERY JOURNAL QUESTIONS

1. Think about your creative life. Has it been negatively affected by your patterns of use and by your addictive tendencies? Have you produced less as you've used more? Have you produced inferior work because you aren't sufficiently present and because you're always rushing through your work in order to get to the bottle or some other fix?
2. If these profound negative consequences haven't occurred yet, can you read the handwriting on the wall?
3. Do you want to sacrifice your creative life in the service of your

addiction, or would you prefer to honor your creative nature
and fight the addiction?

CREATIVE-RECOVERY EXERCISES

1. Look up AA or some other recovery program on the Internet. A search will provide innumerable sites to explore. Take a several-hour journey into the world of self-help groups, doing your best to stay open-minded. When you are done, patiently appraise what you have learned and decide whether attending one or another of the available meetings might be something to consider.
2. Think through whether the LifeRing Secular Recovery construct of an inner sober voice and an inner addict voice captures something of your internal dynamic. If it does, transcribe one of those conversations and become better acquainted with each voice: how it argues, what it wants, and (for the addict voice especially) what tricks It pulls.

Practicing Awareness

A significant early task in the recovery process is to pay attention to recovery. This means that you put recovery at the top of the list of the things that you remain mindful about, in recognition of the fact that the rest of your life will not work if you are an active addict. You wake up remembering that you are working a recovery program and that this is another day of working that program. You go to bed remembering that you are working a recovery program and evaluate to what extent you kept to your program or put yourself at risk. Recovery becomes the staple of your mental landscape.

You pay attention by keeping a creative-recovery journal. You pay attention by joining a twelve-step group or other self-help group and by making real and regular use of it. You pay attention by noticing your habits, your behaviors, and your relationship to risk and temptation. In these and in the ways we are about to describe, you never let your addiction or your recovery slip very far from your attention. You remember that *recovery always comes first*. Here are six practical suggestions to help you practice awareness.

1. Become a cognitive expert

Bravely notice what you're thinking, dispute any unproductive thoughts, especially those that jeopardize your recovery, and substitute more productive or affirmative language for your unproductive or negative thinking. Notice yourself thinking, "That cold beer looks good"; immediately remind yourself that an innocent thought like that is also, for you, dangerous and unwanted; and substitute "I think I'll have a nice cold bottled water." Get a grip on your mind by noticing what you are saying to yourself and by disputing any self-talk that jeopardizes your recovery.

2. Become an anxiety expert

Learn how your anxiety manifests itself. Maybe it manifests itself by causing you to start lots of creative projects but not complete many. Maybe it manifests itself in your disparaging self-talk. Learn where your anxiety resides and how it shows its face. Then learn how to manage it. You might use deep-breathing techniques, cognitive techniques, behavioral techniques (such as systematic desensitization), guided-visualization techniques (picturing yourself in a calm place), relaxation techniques (massaging your shoulder), discharge techniques (silently screaming so as to dissipate anxiety), or something of your own devising that reduces your experience of anxiety. Learning how to reduce your anxiety is a vital part of your work.

3. Become a meaning expert

Recognize that you must take charge of making and maintaining the meaning in your life, a task that involves making decisions about what will constitute meaningful work and noticing when the meaning leaks out of something (for instance, out of your current novel). You want to recognize clearly that a meaning crisis can threaten your sobriety and learn how to make meaning investments by, for example, holding the concert that you're about to play as meaningful even though you don't get to celebrate it with heroin. The more clearly you come to understand how meaning comes and goes and what you can do—what you must do—to recapture it when it leaks away, the better your chances for a solid recovery.

4. Become an emotions expert

Notice your feelings. Notice that you have feelings! When you receive a piece of toxic criticism from a literary agent, gallery owner, or other marketplace player, notice how that makes you feel—and find a way to ventilate those feelings. If you try to act as if you haven't felt anything or if you try to stuff those feelings away, you put yourself at risk for using. Learn to detach from your feelings by saying, "I am feeling sad and disappointed right this second, but I am more than my feelings. My feelings do not define me." Have your feelings, honor your feelings, and also *deal with* your feelings in direct, immediate, and productive ways.

5. Become a risk-assessment expert

Does the opening of one of your painting shows always make you tremen-dously anxious? Then the opening coming up next Tuesday is dangerous business, and you want to acknowledge honestly the extent to which it is tempting you to use. Tell someone how dangerous the reception is feeling, how anxious it is making you, and how much you want to drink to deal with your anxiety. Do not turn a blind eye to risk, even though a part of you wants to do exactly that—since risk is also an opportunity to use. Even in the most ordinary and innocent situations, remember to ask yourself, "Is anything here going to jeopardize my sobriety?"

6. Take charge of your attitude

You can turn everything into a big drama, secretly knowing that you are going to need a few drinks to deal with that sudden tumult—or you can stop that dramatizing. You can act like the most beleaguered, stressed-out, put-upon person in the world—or you can stop that unhelpful self-representing. You can never smile, never laugh, never enjoy, never feel good, and never love—or you can change your attitude. A large part of the work of recovery is deciding who you want to be and then becoming that person.

Mindfulness Practice

How do you become a cognitive expert, an anxiety expert, a meaning ex-pert, and so on? The short answer is by paying better attention and by routinely acknowledging your thoughts and feelings. For instance, you know that you are anxious because you have been paying attention to your body and acknowledging your anxious thoughts and feelings. A great way to learn to pay better attention is through what is known as mindfulness practice. A mindfulness practice provides a way to pause and check in with yourself about what you're thinking and feeling.

You don't need to engage in a lengthy daily meditation practice to achieve mindfulness. It's our belief that just ten seconds of mindful breathing and checking in can be truly beneficial. The idea is to use a single deep breath as a container for a specific thought. First you practice deep breathing until you can produce a breath that lasts about five seconds on the inhale and five seconds on the exhale. Then you couple this deep breath with a useful phrase designed to promote awareness.

In meditation, traditionally the goal is no thinking. In the practice we're describing, we would like you to insert a thought into that deep breath, silently thinking half of the thought on the inhale and half of the thought on the exhale. These breath-and-thought bundles can become incantations (a word from magic that means the ritual recitation of a verbal charm) that help open you up to acknowledging your problem. The magical effects of these particular incantations are instant calm and more truthful thinking.

We humans usually avoid deep breathing because it slows us down to such an extent that we are forced to confront the truth of our situation. A vicious cycle evolves where we maintain shallow breathing as a defense against knowing our own thoughts. If we are willing to engage in conscious deep breathing, we instantly become more mindful and begin to see our tricks, dodges, and dependencies. So deep breathing, in and of itself, is a wonderful awareness practice, one that you can master right now. There is nothing arcane to learn, no long sitting meditations to endure, no distinctions to make between emptying your mind versus concentrating deeply. You simply practice taking one long, deep breath, a breath longer and fuller than the breath you usually experience. Practice this sort of deep breathing right now.

Next we'd like you to add certain useful phrases. The thrust of cognitive therapy is that what we say to ourselves—our self-talk—is the primary way that we maintain our problems, defenses, flaws, blocks, and addictions. If we manage to change our self-talk, we have done something profound, something more substantial than just making a few innocent linguistic changes. This new self-talk creates new grooves in the brain and reinforces the recovery process; now, when we think one of our customary thoughts, it is a positive, life-affirming, counteraddictive thought.

Following are some incantations that create an opening through which the truth about your situation can enter and that help you talk yourself into a better relationship with your addiction problems. We've used parentheses to indicate how each incantation naturally divides between the inhale and the exhale (but if these divisions don't work for you, find a natural break for yourself). Give these two sets of four incantations each a try right now, remembering to drop each incantation into a single long, deep breath. In a moment we'll explain when to use Set 1 and when to use Set 2.

SET 1
(I am completely) (stopping)
(I am open) (to knowing)
(I am equal) (to the truth)
(I return) (with strength)

SET 2
(I am completely) (stopping)
(I acknowledge) (my problem)

(I accept) (my responsibilities)
(I return) (with strength)

It is very hard to use a technique like this consistently or to begin and maintain a fruitful inner dialogue if you don't set aside time for it or provide a structure for it. So we hope that you will do the following: Each morning, set aside five minutes. Begin this five-minute interval by incanting (breathing and thinking) "I am completely stopping," as stopping your mind chatter and your rush through life is always a good first step. If you are just beginning your investigation of your relationship to addiction or are still debating whether you have a problem with an addiction, next incant "I am open to knowing" and then "I am equal to the truth." Then use the remainder of your five-minute mindfulness practice to learn from yourself—by journaling, by drawing, or just by thinking—whatever you need to know about your addiction.

When you've completed your five-minute practice, incant "I return with strength" to bring yourself back. Continue with the rest of your day as you hold in awareness any conclusions you reached about your addiction. Notice any budding intentions and any thoughts you may have about how you want to address your addiction. Keep a pad with you (or the electronic equivalent) and begin to record your thoughts and intentions. In this way, you carry over your morning mindfulness practice throughout the day, living a life richer in awareness and shorter on denial.

If you already know that you are having problems with an addiction, then instead of using the incantations "I am completely stopping," "I am open to knowing," and "I am equal to the truth," use "I am completely stopping," "I acknowledge my problem," and "I accept my responsibilities." These three incantations, used repeatedly as the opening salvo of your battle against your addiction, keep denial and defensiveness from returning, reduce your need to use, and remind you of your intention to live soberly and authentically. Follow these three incantations with five minutes of useful recovery work, such as selecting an afternoon AA meeting or choosing a new place to eat lunch where you won't encounter your drinking buddies.

As a creative person, you may want to move directly from this five-minute mindfulness practice to your creative work. After your brief practice, turn right to your novel, your painting, or your composing. There are several good reasons to do this: to use any sleep thinking you might have done during the night, to experience making some meaning first thing in the day, and to build the habit of regular daily creating. In the picture we're painting, you would start your day mindfully acknowledging your addiction problems or doing some other important recovery work, and then you would segue directly to a good stint of creative work. Can you really think of a better scenario for the first hour or two of your day?

Creative Exercises

Increasing your awareness so that you are more ready to acknowledge your addiction problems is the theme of this chapter's creative-exercise practice. We suggest that you incorporate what you've learned so far about yourself, your addictive tendencies, your defenses, and using your creative nature in the service of self-awareness in doing these exercises.

For example, try applying the mindfulness technique of nonjudgmental observation first to your own responses to the *idea* of doing the exercises and then to the experience of actually *doing* the exercises. What differences do you notice? What does that tell you about the feeling of avoiding doing something versus doing something?

1. For the writer in you

Write a short story in which one character is more mindful than every-one else around him. What strikes you about his demeanor? How does he respond to the people around him and vice versa? Reread your story and learn from your own intuition and artistry what mindfulness looks like.

2. For the visual artist in you

Make a collage in which the elephant in the room (the problem or issue that is felt but not seen or acknowledged) is both clearly visible and also hard to locate. Reflect on how something similar might occur in your own life: how an addiction might at once be perfectly obvious and also some-how hidden. Describe your responses to that collage.

3. For the actor in you

Visualize a character who is very truthful in general, who may even pride herself on her truthfulness, but who is in denial with respect to her ad-diction. How would you portray such a character in her everyday life, priding herself on her truthfulness while also defending herself against this one big truth? What does it feel like to live in this person's skin? What part of this character's dilemma do you identify with? What would you want that character to do in response to her dilemma? Imagine how you feel if she does or doesn't do that. Attend to your responses.

4. For the scientist in you

Analyze the concept of denial. What does the existence of this core defense say about the way our brain organizes reality and how our species can maintain illusions and delusions? How do you understand this process in your own life? Use this understanding to identify your own areas of denial.

5. For the dreamer in you

Let's say that you have a problem with an addiction and that you've admitted to that problem. In your mind's eye, turn that insight into a series of concrete actions. What would those actions look like? Where do you want that path to take you? What happens when you arrive there? Make note of your responses to your arrival at this special place, describe them to yourself out loud, and write them down in your creative-recovery journal.

Postscript

Maintaining an honest and mindful self-awareness during the course of one's day-to-day life is an ongoing challenge for most of us under the best of circumstances—and much more difficult when we're confronted by an addiction problem. Extra help is needed, help that is spiritual or existential in nature. Come with us as we help you make the existential or spiritual leap into recovery.

6 ⧄ *The Existential or Spiritual Leap*

Once you acknowledge your problem, it's time to take a leap into a new and more honest self-relationship, where the desire to be authentic replaces the idle hope to exert complete control and where a willingness to be human replaces the need to look good at all costs.

Making the existential or spiritual leap in recovery means that you move from an egoistic defensiveness intended to shield you from the reality of your affliction to an acceptance of the demands of personal responsibility. You move from a grandiose individualism to a more authentic individualism that takes into account your strengths and weaknesses, the existence of other people, and the dynamic forces at play in the universe, including the forces contributing to your addiction.

This is most centrally a leap from self-centered pride and isolation to mindfulness and connection to the larger whole. As the anthropologist Gregory Bateson describes it, "The panic of the alcoholic who has hit bottom is the panic of the man who thought he had control over a vehicle but suddenly finds that the vehicle can run away with him. Suddenly, pressure on what he knows is the brake seems to make the vehicle go faster. It is the panic of discovering that 'it' (the system, self plus vehicle) is bigger than he is."

The recognition of that bigness does not squash you as an individual. Rather, it awakens in you the understanding that you are not separate from the universe—not separate from all that is grand and petty, beautiful and ugly, miraculous and ordinary. In its own way it is exactly like the creative leap, where you use your individual talent to make a sincere connection with what is true, beautiful, and good.

Why call this an existential or spiritual leap and not something else? Because in the existential tradition the individual is encouraged to face up to his contingency, to his reality as a precarious human being embedded in and subject to the dynamics of culture and nature. A person's goal, according to the existential view, is not to control life but to make an honest effort in the face of contingent reality. He is encouraged to just be human, which, as the existentialist knows, is a lot to ask of an ordinary person.

Similarly, in the spiritual and religious traditions, the individual is advised to consider herself a part of the universe rather than separate from the universe. Her central task is to align with the natural order and the dictates of the many profound forces operating in and regulating the universe. Likewise, she is encouraged to leap from an egocentric isolationism to cosmic attunement and find fellowship among like-minded souls who, like her, stand in praise of something other than, and more than, the individual ego.

The existential or spiritual leap is a leap to the acceptance of contingency and participation: that you are simply human and that you manifest your humanity by participating with integrity in the project of your life. Whether you believe in the supernatural or the accidental, you are faced with the same mandate: to get over yourself and take the wider, humbler, and truer view, that you have no iron grip on anything and that manifesting a quiet courage in the face of contingency is the noble path.

What will help you make this leap? Maybe you suddenly understand that the networks in your brain have crossed over into addiction. Maybe you're beginning to experience the painful negative consequences of your out-of-control behavior—for instance, when your wife serves you with divorce papers or your boss threatens to fire you. Maybe you've begun to see how your drug use really isn't helping you write those brilliant screenplays you still believe are in you. Maybe you've hit bottom, or maybe you can see that bottom coming. Whatever causes you to make that leap, once you accept your connection to everything that is, you become filled with a wonderful and necessary humility, a humility arising from the recognition that you are exactly and precisely human.

What does this leap sound like? It sounds like the movement from "I will do whatever I want!" to "I will do the right thing." It sounds like the movement from "I can control anything I set my mind to!" to "I will make a genuine effort to honor my obligations and walk my path with heart." It sounds like the movement from "The world revolves around me!" to "I am subjectively important, but my code of conduct requires me to take others into account." It is a leap in the direction of taking responsibility for your actions toward others and, if you are a believer, toward your God. It is also a leap in the direction of a less grandiose way of creating: that is, a leap in the direction of more creating and fewer theatrics.

People construe this leap in very different ways. Some will see it as a new, better individualism that allows for meaningful connections with their fellow human beings. Some will see it as the long-anticipated return to the belief system of their childhood. Some will see it as the way to translate their spiritual feelings into concrete behaviors and a way of life. What each version of this leap will share in common, if it is the actual leap, is a willingness to surrender to the reality of addiction and the necessity of personal responsibility and meaningful connection with others.

Agnostics and atheists in recovery often establish connection to this larger whole by invoking beliefs in science or art, in the centrality of family, in the fellowship of recovering people, in dedication to the creative process, or in the philosophy of personal meaning making. A belief in doing the next right thing can provide a secular view of a power greater than oneself, and atheists who attend Alcoholics Anonymous have been known to comfortably take the concept of God to mean Good Orderly Direction. For them the leap is existential and not spiritual or religious, but no less profound for that.

For the religious in recovery, making the leap usually means accepting a traditional definition of God as promulgated by a specific faith. For those who are spiritual but not religious, that power greater than oneself may be defined as nature, some universal force such as love or divine intelligence, or the compassion and loving-kindness of the Buddhists. The researcher Keith Humphreys defines spirituality as "an individual's personal sense of the sacred and its relationship to ultimate concerns like the meaning of existence, morality, suffering, and death," and in that light spirituality need not be related to any particular god or religious tradition.

Whether you are existential, secular, religious, or spiritual, your goals are to learn to connect with the larger whole—whether you frame that as the universe or as the human condition—and to integrate all aspects of your authentic self, including your shadow side of guilt and shame and your unacceptable thoughts, feelings, and behaviors. You endeavor to maintain meaning, authenticity, and connection, including the connection to your creative work, while at the same time not falling for the false promise of an addictive shortcut.

We are talking much more about willingness than willpower. Carlo DiClemente states: "Very successful talk-show hosts, athletes, actors, comedians, and businesspersons have become addicted, suffered significant losses, and found change difficult, if not impossible. Certainly these individuals had the willpower, dedication, and commitment to become successful. Changing addictive behaviors takes more than simple willpower." If it is willingness and not willpower that you need, what sort of willingness is it? It is the willingness to surrender: to the reality of your mere humanity, to the reality of your addictive nature, and to the reality that you must now engage in process—the recovery process—and not in wishful thinking.

In this regard, Stephanie Brown explains: "Surrender is the moment of accepting reality on the unconscious level. The individual knows the deepest truth, regardless of wishes or explanations to the contrary. Defenses used in the service of denying that reality no longer work. The individual who has accepted the reality of loss of control can proceed to live with that reality, beginning the process of recovery." When you surrender and admit to the facts of existence, you take a giant step in the direction of assuming personal responsibility for your thoughts, your actions, your creativity, and your recovery.

You are surrendering to the fact that you have feelings, that you can't control as much as you thought you could control, that you have limitations, and that you may have been shamed in life or may have shamed yourself. This last needs special clarification. There is an important difference between healthy shame that translates as "I made a mistake" and allows you to ask for help and toxic shame that translates as "I *am* a mistake" and results in further denial and avoidance. A recovering addict who fails to understand the distinction between healthy shame and toxic shame tends to have a hard time working through the perceived stigma of identifying as an addict in recovery. Surrender to the fact that you may have made mistakes, but do not think for a second that you *are* a mistake.

Your leap toward acceptance of the limits of the human and the reality of the power of addiction is likely to land you in one of the self-help recovery groups we discussed in the previous chapter, groups such as Alcoholics Anonymous, LifeRing, Women for Sobriety, or some informal neighborhood or workplace support group comprising sober people. In these settings your leap is likely to be formally supported by the structure and tenets of the program.

In AA, for example, building on an acknowledgment in Step 1 that you are powerless over alcohol, you are encouraged to use Steps 2 and 3 to address the issue of taking the existential or spiritual leap. Step 2 (coming to believe that a power greater than ourselves can restore us to sanity) and Step 3 (making a decision to turn our will and our lives over to the care of God as we understand him) offer a way out of despair by establishing authentic attachment to the larger system in which you exist. As we discussed earlier, this power greater than ourselves or God may be construed in existential, secular, religious, or spiritual terms.

According to researchers such as Diane Davis and Golie Jansen, this special sense of powerlessness is "very different from the meanings of powerlessness associated with contemporary social and behavioral science, such as alienation, anomie, victimization, oppression, discrimination, and poverty." AA is not trying to discourage already-discouraged people; rather, it is trying to promote an acceptance of powerlessness over addiction as transformational, as part of a "power from within" model rather than a "power over others" model. This is akin to the paradoxical experience of gaining control by first relinquishing it.

LifeRing, by contrast, does not deny its members a spiritual or religious life but does argue that belief is irrelevant for recovery. While they accept the importance of sobriety and of relationships among recovering people, they eschew concepts of surrender and powerlessness. Whereas AA works to deflate an addict's grandiose ego, LifeRing attempts to empower its members by emphasizing personal responsibility and self-reliance. In LSR, taking the existential step primarily involves taking personal responsibility for sobriety. While asserting the desirability of connecting to the larger system of recovering people, LifeRing maintains a singular focus on the existential concepts of authenticity and personal responsibility.

You can see by the differences between AA and LSR that your existential or spiritual leap can come in quite different flavors. It may feel like a turning toward God; it may feel like a turning toward your own authentic nature. It may feel like a gentle embrace as you move fluidly in a direction you have long wanted to move, or it may feel like a real wrenching as you shed some of your grandiosity, arrogance, and lifelong defenses. It is at once a softening and a toughening, a softening to the limits of the human and a toughening in the direction of personal responsibility. It may feel more like one or more like the other, but it is actually both— both a gentle thing and something quite steely.

No doubt you learned a long time ago that you ought not exert rigid control over your paintings, your songs, or your poetry, because operating with an iron hand tends to kill off invention and inspiration and result in formulaic work. You've probably learned how to surrender in your art and how to live with the surprises that emerge, some of them wonderful, some of them not so wonderful. Now you have a new sort of surrendering to learn and to experience as you make the existential or spiritual leap into your full, beautiful, and painful humanness.

CREATIVE-RECOVERY JOURNAL QUESTIONS

1. Imagine the existential or spiritual leap as a leap to integration. What does framing it that way suggest to you?

> 2. How can an admission of powerlessness be the first step in the assumption of responsibility? Try not to move past this point until you have satisfied yourself that this idea makes sense. If you can't satisfy yourself on this score, at least hold the intention that you will revisit the idea of an appropriate surrender to the facts of existence.

CREATIVE-RECOVERY EXERCISES

1. Articulate this existential or spiritual leap for yourself. What are you leaping from and what are you leaping to? Imagine that you have made this leap. Carefully articulate your new stance in life by creating two lists, one of the new behaviors that you want to support, one of the old behaviors that you want to extinguish.
2. Let's say that you can't quite make this leap yet. In that case, create a plan that will help you make the leap at some point in the near future. What steps are required to promote this leap?

Making the Leap

Following are two case studies that illustrate how individuals find meaningful ways to connect to the larger whole in recovery. Rodney may be said to have made the existential leap in early recovery, while Hilda made the spiritual leap at a later point in her ongoing recovery.

The Case of Rodney

Rodney R., a forty-four-year-old divorced scientist and self-identified atheist, came to see Susan complaining of sleepwalking. He had seriously injured himself falling down a short flight of stairs one night and was referred to therapy by his emergency room doctor.

Rodney told Susan that his girlfriend had expressed concern about his sleepwalking several months earlier, but until the accident he had not taken her concerns seriously. As the story unfolded, the cause of Rodney's fall became increasingly clear. Sleepwalking was not the problem. Going down the stairs in the dark while loaded on Valium was the problem.

Apparently Rodney had started taking prescription pills for anxiety two years earlier, while he was going through a divorce. Although he had a family history of alcoholism, he had never been a big drinker and prided himself on his lack of interest in substances while in college and graduate school. When he began taking Valium, at first he used it only a couple of times a week, just when he felt he needed it. Within six months he was using it daily but didn't think twice about it, as his doctor continued to prescribe it.

Rodney admitted that there were often times when he ran out of pills and had to order more off the Internet, but he nevertheless didn't see that as a problem. His physician kept refilling his prescriptions, seemingly clueless about the extent of Rodney's use. Rodney had become accustomed by then to lying to his doctor regularly and found himself taking larger and larger quantities of pills.

Rodney's therapy over the next few months focused on his chronic sense of emptiness, his loneliness, and his addiction to pills. Susan referred him to a chemical-dependency outpatient program, since he needed a medical detox and more structure, and finally he accepted and made use of the referral. He left individual therapy at that point and went to a chemical-dependency group program for six months.

By the time Rodney returned to individual therapy with Susan, he had been clean for eight months and was regularly attending Narcotics Anonymous meetings. He explained that even though he was hesitant at first because of his problem with "the God thing" at the meetings, he had met a fellow scientist who was agnostic and who helped Rodney translate the twelve-step motto "God as you understand him" into existential terms.

Rodney explained that for the first time in his life he felt some real relief from his pervasive sense of emptiness and chronic loneliness by fashioning an authentic relationship with his higher power and learning to rely on that power. He didn't recite the customary Lord's Prayer at the end of the meetings and steered clear of the meetings in which overtly religious people sometimes dominated the discussion. He found an NA home group where his fellow members were more spiritual than religious; no one seemed to judge him, and he began to take active responsibility for his quality of life in sobriety.

The Case of Hilda

Hilda W., a choral singer, had seen a lot in her life. Susan could read that in her face and in the rigid way she held her body. She was a seventy-year-old German who had been a child during the bombings in Dresden and who still startled easily. She had come to the United States in the 1950s, gotten married, had two children, lost her husband to cancer in her early sixties, and become an alcoholic soon thereafter.

Susan first met Hilda when she came into a long-term recovery group, at which point she had been sober for about four months. Her adult children had chided her into getting sober, initially by threatening her access to her grandchildren. When she saw that she had actually started to feel better sober, she kept her program going on her own.

Hilda identified herself as religious and as a Lutheran but seemed to get little comfort from her faith. She shared with Susan that her father had been a lay minister before the war, and she equated her childhood religion with the cold, authoritarian severity he embodied. Singing hymns with her mother and at church had been about the only pleasurable activity allowed her. Her father left the family to go to war and never returned.

Along with her neighborhood friends, Hilda was coerced into becoming a member of the Hitler Youth. By the time the war ended, she had pretty much stopped singing. She was self-reliant, accustomed to severe deprivation, and emotionally as hard as nails. Alcohol provided the only relief available and was by far the most reliable.

The therapists in Hilda's early-recovery group had encouraged her to try Alcoholics Anonymous, but she was adamant about not setting foot in a meeting, as she imagined the program would replicate the same austere hierarchy in which she was raised. In addition, she was tightly defended against any feelings of vulnerability or dependency, and she didn't like being told what to do by anyone.

Despite her tendency to reject help, as she found help humiliating, she continued with a long-term recovery group after she graduated from the first phase of the program. During the course of her first two years of recovery work, Hilda began to gain access to her emotions. She started to learn to express herself to this small circle of people whom she was beginning to trust. Although she remained guarded more often than not, she started to find moments of genuine connection within the group, including the ability to resolve conflicts with the group members. She began to reach out more to her adult children, who seemed receptive to her overtures, especially as she was staying sober.

In her third year in the recovery group, Hilda began attending Life-Ring Secular Recovery meetings on a regular basis, to the pleasant surprise of the group leaders. She made friends with a couple of women at the meetings and started socializing with them outside of therapy. Life-Ring's philosophy does not focus on religion or spirituality in recovery, but Hilda nevertheless became interested in attending Unitarian church services with one of her new friends.

She became a regular participant at this new church and, for the first time in her life, got exposed to a variety of nonrigid spiritual approaches. She began to see how her previous views about religion had limited her. She even joined the church choir after years away from singing. It took Hilda much trial and error to find a meaningful connection to the larger whole, but eventually she was able to take this spiritual step into a more loving way of life in recovery. She began slowly healing the traumas of her youth, allowing others to assist her along the way.

As you can see from Rodney's and Hilda's stories, taking the existential or spiritual leap can prove to be hard work. This sort of change typically does not happen on its own and requires self-investigation and conscious effort. Let's now look at some ways that you can make this leap possible.

Regular Mindfulness Practice

The leap that we've been talking about can also be thought of as a leap from unjustified, stubborn pride and delusion to mindfulness. To consolidate the gains you make after leaping, you want to pay real attention to your behaviors, attitudes, and emotional states. This careful attention can amount to a regular practice, the same sort of regular practice that creative clients learn to maintain to keep themselves in right relationship to their creative efforts. Maintaining a mindfulness practice or creative practice will help you maintain your sobriety. Let's look at what your daily mindfulness practice might include.

When someone says that she maintains a spiritual practice, we have an intuitive sense of what that person means and what that practice might entail. We envision her engaging in certain activities in a ceremonial way, whether that is lighting candles or sitting meditatively; we expect that she spends a certain amount of time every day, probably first thing each morning, formally engaged with her practice; and we picture her practice informing all aspects of her life, such that, for instance, when a crisis occurs, she uses her belief set (about an afterlife, say) and her techniques (like prayer or meditation) to see her through the crisis.

Likewise, if someone tells us that he is training for a marathon, a boxing match, or a high-altitude climb, we immediately get a picture of what that includes. We expect that he exercises every day, even on days that he doesn't want to exercise; that he watches his diet and takes a pass on the hot fudge sundaes, even though he craves them; and that he visualizes success and talks himself into the right frame of mind. We picture him taking charge of his mind and his body and engaging in a goal-oriented process that naturally includes pushing himself in ways that, on many days, he may actually hate.

Martial artists provide another model. We picture their formality: the way they bow when they enter the martial arts studio and when they face an opponent before a match. We picture their intensity: the way they shout, the way they drive themselves, the way they focus on a given move and a given routine. We picture the value system by which they operate, which revolves around the honorable use of force and sanctifies self-control, including the self-control to walk away rather than to fight.

Then there's the path of the dedicated thinker, someone who lives for intellectual problems to solve and whose main meaning investments have to do with unraveling the laws of the universe, finding cures for diseases, or inventing ever-better mousetraps. In this case, we picture a self-directed person who takes it upon himself to pick his path, even if it runs counter to the path his peers are following; to bite into his problem as a starving man bites into a juicy sandwich; and to demonstrate a tenacity that is sometimes punctuated by joyous shrieks of "Eureka!"

And what if someone tells us that she has spent a lifetime battling for the rights and the release of political prisoners? In our mind's eye we see her engaged in a dedicated, daily way, in the face of setbacks and indifference, with an enterprise whose details she doesn't necessarily love but one that she is convinced is important and righteous. We don't picture her smiling much; we don't picture her life punctuated by that many prisoner releases; but we understand why she is bringing every ounce of her fortitude to this enterprise.

We would like you to construct a mindfulness practice that incorporates core elements from these models. Rather than live your life and engage in recovery in a hit-or-miss way, without sufficient motivation, energy, or regularity, you can construct a routine that minimizes your disinclination to pay attention and maximizes your natural abilities, your personality strengths, and your creative nature. In the previous chapter, we advised you to start out each day with a five-minute mindfulness interval. Now we want to ask you to do a little more.

Begin your day with those five minutes of mindfulness, using the incantations that we described in the previous chapter. Then go on to your creative work for an hour or two (to make time for this, you may have to get up very early). Then end your morning practice with a longer mindfulness stint, maybe on the order of fifteen or twenty minutes, during which you pay careful attention to your recovery needs. This might entail writing in your creative-recovery journal, doing one of our exercises, planning your sober day, or working one of the steps of the self-help programs.

Your practice—the first stint of mindfulness, the period of creativity, and the second stint of mindfulness—is something that over time you will see as the very best way to start your day and the very best way to honor your recovery and your creativity. To ensure that this practice functions as well as it can, you will want to imbue it with the following twelve elements. You may want to turn these elements into a list that you keep on prominent display in your morning practice space, to remind you of what this practice can and ought to feel like.

1. Simplicity

Your life may be complex, but your practice can be simple. It is as simple as showing up. It is as simple as saying "I will not drink today" and meaning it. It is as simple as learning how to abstain by abstaining. It is so simple that it can be said in a very few words. For instance, you hold the thought "I will not drink today," and you do not drink today. You hold the thought "I am perfectly fine without a drink," and you proceed to live your day without alcohol. You hold a simple thought, and you take daily action in support of that goal.

2. Regularity

Your practice requires that you practice every day. You do not skip your practice because it is gloomy out or because you are gloomy inside. You pledge to show up every day and pay attention to your commitment to not drinking—and then you honor that pledge. Every day means every day: that is the essence of regularity. You hold the thought "sober today"; if you are resistant to that thought, you stop everything and recommit to your intention to abstain. If you find yourself in the middle of a crisis, very busy, quite tired, or anything at all, you nevertheless turn in a regular, nondramatic way to your intention to remain sober.

3. Solemnity

You engage in your practice because it matters to you and because life, and those aspects of life like sobriety that you intend to honor, are not a joke. Your practice is meaningful; it is respectful of the vision you hold for yourself; it is one of the primary ways you show your heroism, your humanity, and your love of life. Because you hold it in this high esteem, you treat it seriously. If in fact your sobriety doesn't matter to you on a given day, you stop everything and recommit to your recovery. You are not joyless in your pursuit of recovery, but you are definitely serious in your intentions.

4. Honesty

Your mindfulness practice amounts to little if you are not honest. If you feel the pressure building to drink, you are honest and say, "Trouble brewing." Then you immediately do what you have learned to do when your drinking obsession returns. You honestly acknowledge that it may take all of your resources to maintain your sobriety; you are honest about the effort involved and about the negative consequences if you permit yourself to slip. You are not honest for the sake of taking some perverse joy in your flaws and blemishes; you are honest so that you can rise to the level of your aspirations.

5. Right Self-Direction

You take responsibility, in a completely nongrandiose way, for guiding your practice and your recovery program. Although you need to stay humble and learn from others, you fundamentally make your own decisions. You guide yourself through the process with an open heart, watching out for the blandishments of ego and the limitations of willpower. You listen carefully to others—to people who speak at twelve-step meetings, to your doctor, to addiction experts—but you decide for yourself what constitutes your best practices. When you do not know what to do, you search out solutions and not excuses. It ultimately rests on your shoulders.

6. Right Intensity

You can exercise lackadaisically or you can exercise intensely. You can write your screenplay in an absent way or with real commitment. You can care only a little about your efforts or you can care a lot about them. The same is true with respect to your approach to recovery. You can bring your full wattage or you can bring only a fraction of your passion and energy. Your practice demands full intensity: every muscle fiber, every moral conviction, and every brain cell. This is especially true because you have so many pulls to addiction, including the pulls provided by your very individuality. You can only best such an adversary with real effort.

7. Presence

When you want to pay attention to being sober, you want to pay real attention. You don't want to be half thinking about the bills that need paying or half thinking about your child's grade point average. You especially don't want to be half thinking about drinking. You want to shake off distractions, quiet your nerves, silence your mind chatter, and be in real contact with your desire to remain sober. When you take a plane trip, you want your pilot to be thinking about nothing but landing the plane; you want your surgeon to be thinking about nothing but sewing you up correctly. Likewise you want to be completely present for the work directly in front of you, the work of remaining sober.

8. Ceremony

You want to go about your practice in a ceremonial way, giving it an added measure of respect and poignancy. You can begin your practice absently, attend to it absently, and leave it absently, or you can imbue it with the same ceremonial feel that accompanies your stage performance or the way you carefully clean your paintbrushes. Unlike a wedding, a confirmation, or a funeral, your practice does not come with any built-in sense of ceremony: you must add that ingredient.

9. Joy

Your practice can bring you great joy. It can bring you joy in several ways: in the experience of living mindfully, in the pride you take in heroically meeting your commitments, and in the sobriety you maintain. It may not bring you joy every day, and on some days it will feel like nothing but work. But on other days a surge of joy will rise up in you as you appreciate your efforts at authentic living. Joy can attend to your practice, even if it manifests itself as rarely as sunny days during a spell of bad weather. Remember that joy is nearby and invite that joy in.

10. Discipline

Discipline is the muscle of your practice. Each bit of attention that you pay to your practice, every extra minute that you spend with it, each time you turn to it, is both the measure of your discipline and the way you build your muscles. Discipline helps you crack through resistance; it allows you to stay put even when you feel anxious and uncomfortable; it aids your quick recovery after slips. Every act of clear intention in support of your practice, even the smallest one, strengthens the foundation upon which your sobriety is being built.

11. Self-Trust

You need to trust, in a non-egotistic, nonnarcissistic, and nongrandiose way, that you have the internal resources to maintain your commitments. If you're sure that you're going to fail, if you're certain that you can only be strong for a little while, if you're convinced that you really can't live without alcohol, you've added powerful obstacles to success. This self-trust is an element of your practice: you bring to your practice a profound belief in your *choice* to remain sober and a profound belief in your *ability* to remain sober. Over time, by maintaining your practice and by maintaining your sobriety, you earn the self-trust you have been affirming daily.

12. Primacy

Many things in life are important, but few require the attention and work that recovering from an addiction does. It is really your primary concern, because of the way not paying attention to your addiction can ruin your life. Therefore your practice should reflect this core importance. Your practice stands at the top of your to-do list, not somewhere in the middle. You don't skip your practice because something has come up. You attend to it rather than to less-important things. You give it early-morning primacy and moment-to-moment primacy in your life: it is that important.

CREATIVE-RECOVERY EXERCISE

Envision your mindfulness practice. Imagine incorporating the twelve elements we discussed above. What do you expect this sort of practice to feel like? How can this sort of practice help your recovery? Spend some time visualizing your mindfulness practice.

Creative Exercises

Now enlist your creativity to help you make the existential or spiritual leap into sobriety and recovery. This is a good place to practice mindfulness as you observe the way you think and feel about doing the exercises—before, during, and after you do them. As before, feel free to make notes in your creative-recovery journal about your responses to this process.

1. For the writer in you

Write a scene set at a twelve-step or other support-group meeting that depicts a character suddenly getting what surrender means. Describe what changes for that character internally and externally. Does this shift affect how your character relates to others at the meeting? How so? Notice your own responses to this character both before and after the shift. What are the implications for you? How can you make use of these observations personally?

2. For the visual artist in you

Paint this existential or spiritual leap, paying special attention to the landing. Notice what it was like for you to paint this picture. Which part was easier, the leap or the landing? Describe what you are landing *on* and how you feel about it. How can you incorporate this into your recovery process?

3. For the musician in you

Write a song that captures the moment before leaping, the leap, and the moment after leaping. What key best fits this song? What's the tempo? When you have finished, perform your song—in the mirror and, if possible, in front of an audience. Observe your responses to the various elements of the song. How does it feel to perform it alone? How does it feel to perform it in front of others? What have you learned about the process of acceptance and surrender?

4. For the scientist in you

Carefully distinguish between an existential leap and a spiritual leap. What factors are involved in each of them? Do the factor analysis. Can they ever amount to the same thing or are they fundamentally different? Which factors do you most strongly respond to personally, either positively or negatively? Why? Notice your response.

5. For the dreamer in you

Imagine that you've become highly productive at your art—and that you've also transcended your ego. What would that look like? What do you gain? What are you afraid of losing? Imagine yourself accepting your new state. Mindfully notice how you feel about it.

Postscript

After doing this chapter's creative exercises, consider what you now know about yourself regarding taking an existential or spiritual leap into recovery. Be curious as to why you chose the exercises you did and passed on the others. Were there some, for example, that you couldn't bring your-self to do even though in doing them you might have explored some-thing new about yourself?

Without judgment (as best you can) mindfully notice where you find yourself putting on the brakes in taking the leap into recovery. Notice al-ternately what helps you with the process of leaping with confidence. Allow yourself to focus fully on where you want to land in recovery and how you want to empower your creative nature. Once you've done this, turn with us to chapter 7, where we explain how you can employ your creative nature in the recovery process.

7 *Your Creative Nature*

Throughout this book we've been offering you ways that you can employ your creative abilities and your creative nature as aids in understanding and acknowledging your addiction. Now we would like you to use those same abilities and that same nature in the service of your recovery.

Art and Healing

Let's start with the simple idea that making art can heal. This represents a time-honored understanding of the power of creativity, and it explains why the arts have always found a place at the table wherever healing, rehabilitation, and recovery are promoted.

Trauma victims are encouraged to make art. Patients in mental institutions are encouraged to make art, to such an extent that their efforts have led to a branch of art known as outsider art. The field of art therapy sprang up based on the twin ideas that art media can be used for diagnostic purposes and that the use of art media promotes insight and healing.

Beth Malchus of the Ohio Department of Health's Sexual Assault and Domestic Violence Prevention Program states, "There has been a call in the sexual assault and domestic violence movement for the past eight years to use art or creativity to assist with vicarious trauma, secondary trauma stress, and compassion fatigue. There is a large community of rape prevention educators and advocates that knits. In my office during conference calls or when we're under a lot of stress, we color premade mandalas. We have also expanded the definition of creativity beyond painting, composing, or writing: we are relearning that it can be gardening or cooking or planning a party—all is creative. It is a means of reconnecting heart and spirit in what we do." Expressing your thoughts and feelings by drawing, writing, sewing, or in some similar way aids in the recovery process by virtue of the healing properties of making art.

Dr. Michael Samuels, author of *Creative Healing: How to Heal Yourself By Tapping Your Hidden Creativity,* says: "Scientific studies tell us that art heals by changing a person's physiology and attitude. The body's physiology changes from one of stress to one of deep relaxation, from one of fear to one of creativity and inspiration. Making art frees the body's healing mechanisms and unites body, mind, and spirit. In art and healing, no interpretation or therapy is necessary. The creative process is the healer."

For the professional artist who struggles to produce excellent work, to garner sales in the marketplace, and to maintain a career in the arts, making art is not pure process, pure expression, pure joy, or pure healing. It is a much more complicated affair. For the everyday creative person, however, for whom creativity is not driven by excellence or by the marketplace and can bring the same simple joy that drawing brings to a child, writing or crafting can provide a means to express oneself, ventilate feelings, manage anxiety, and heal trauma.

Creating in this simple but important sense—expressing yourself with pastels, writing in your journal—is, among other things, action, and in the context of healing and recovery, taking action in the service of your recovery is better than brooding about your situation. It can be liberating to get your worried thoughts and feelings out as your fingers, heart, and mind work in tandem to produce a quilt, a song, or a poem. It can also open your eyes, as art therapists believe, because you may learn something about your situation when you examine the finished quilt and discover that its pattern and imagery actually reveal something important about your situation.

John, an organizer of Artists Anonymous groups in Australia and a long-time Alcoholics Anonymous sponsor, describes his experience: "I have been in recovery for thirty-two years, and I spent the first twenty years writing an intensive journal of my own devising and doing extensive annual fourth steps [taking a searching and fearless moral inventory]. Nowadays I tell my sponsees to develop their creativity, whatever it may be, because doing something creative is often worth more than repeated fourth steps in blowing away the cobwebs. You can study your navel or you can do some painting, writing, or music and end up with something solid in your hand. A passion is worth far more than introspection!"

John's comments point to another reason that personal expression can prove so valuable in the recovery process. Creating allows for the ventilation of feelings, and it also allows for passion, curiosity, energy, enthusiasm, and love to flow. Many addicts are addicts in part—sometimes in large measure—because they refuse to feel and find it too dangerous to feel. By turning to a blank canvas and announcing that they are about to express themselves, they are doing two curative things at once: agreeing to feel, perhaps for the first time in a long time, and accessing those feelings. This ventilation may likely prove tumultuous and scary, but it can also produce large gains and deep insights.

Marian, a painter, puts it this way:

Nowadays I use my painting as part of my process of healing from depression. My therapist wasn't an art therapist, but he asked me why I didn't paint from my feelings. That set the ball rolling, and I painted over seventy images in five months. I'd drag them along (and they were all big) every week to therapy. The art informed the therapy, enlivened the relationship, and was a key to intuitive insight into my issues.

These pieces were unlike anything I had ever done in my career as an artist and were not meant to be shown. However, my friends and collectors encouraged me to show them. That led to a one-woman university show, which in turn led to the offer of a teaching position. By using my painting skills in this more "real" way, I helped myself heal and, maybe not so oddly, also helped my art career.

It may sound paradoxical to assert that art making can lead to a tumultuous but beneficial release of feelings and also that it can lead to pure relaxation of a sort that is invaluable in the recovery process. Yet both are true. Sometimes our creativity accesses our pain and exorcises our demons and serves us in that way. Sometimes it is a sunny, quiet, meditative sort of thing that serves to reduce our stress and quell our everyday anxious nature. Both are tremendous benefits. You can use your creativity as a tool to help yourself feel and grow, and you can also use it simply to help yourself relax.

Many also argue that your higher power or better self is accessed when you make art. Whether that connection is to some entity that is outside you or to some inner force or knowing, it is nevertheless clear that people regularly experience making art as existentially enriching or spiritually fulfilling. Creating is a time-tested way of acknowledging and including that existential or spiritual component so necessary to the recovery process. As Samuels explains: "Art, prayer, and healing all take us into our inner world, the world of imagery and emotion, of visions and feelings. This journey inward into what used to be called the spirit or soul and is now called the mind is deeply healing."

Most people struggle to maintain a healthy balance between doing and being, between rushing and relaxing, between caring and feeling overwhelmed by the number of things to care about. Art making promotes balance in a number of ways, by slowing time down, by carving a small niche out of a day filled with endless tasks and errands, and by sanctifying those few minutes with personal and perhaps soulful activity. Making art allows for contact with our deeper thoughts and feelings and can quiet the incessant monkey-mind noise percolating in our brain. Recovery is a balancing act; creativity helps maintain that balance.

You can employ traditional modes of expression like writing, painting, singing, and dancing as part of your recovery process. You can use them to ventilate feelings, to reconnect to your heart and your spirit, as a way to communicate with yourself and others about your truth, and as the primary means to explore the root causes of your addiction. You can use art making to relax, to maintain a healthy balance in your life, because it brings you joy, and because expressing yourself is an ego-gratifying, soulful thing to do. You can use your creativity in all of these ways and more.

People feel better when they are creating, even if the process with a given painting, novel, or symphony is painful and difficult, even if they aren't convinced that they are doing excellent work, and even if they dread the marketplace interactions that will follow when their work is done. All of these doubts and difficulties notwithstanding, creative people love creating. Creating is when they feel most alive and most in touch with their thoughts, their feelings, and their authentic self. You can make immediate use of the idea that by doing a little art you can improve your mental health and better meet your challenges by turning to whatever art or craft medium you love—or by turning to one that you would like to get to know better.

CREATIVE-RECOVERY JOURNAL QUESTIONS

1. Have you experienced the healing power of creativity? Can you describe how you might invite that healing power into your recovery process?
2. Is there some art medium that you've wanted to get to know? Might engaging with it now support your recovery?

Creating as Replacement Activity

Creating is not a complete solution to recovering from an addiction. You can write beautifully and write a lot—and still be a practicing alcoholic. You can play the saxophone like a tireless virtuoso—and still be hooked on heroin. Creating is neither the litmus test that proves your wellness nor the key to addiction recovery. The litmus test is actual recovery and actual mental and emotional health.

Indeed, many of the realities of the creative process threaten recovery. If the novel you are working on frustrates you, that frustration threatens your recovery. If you recommit to an acting career but fail to land any interesting roles, that disappointment threatens your recovery. If you rev up your engine in the service of your latest painting and start pouring buckets of adrenaline through your system, that revved-up energy threatens your recovery. Creating can be dangerous.

Nevertheless, creating is also a key to recovery. It is a danger that a creative person must risk. Insofar as creating is one of the truest expressions of your individuality and one of the surest ways to manifest your potential, to give up creating for the sake of a perfectly risk-free recovery is to give up too much. If the choice were between recovery and creativity, you might have to opt for recovery, but that isn't the choice. You can have both recovery and creativity, just so long as you work the steps we suggest and approach your creating in a more mindful way.

As you live your life in recovery, one of your jobs is to engage in activities that replace the behavior associated with your addiction. Previously you spent six hours every night at the bar. Now what will you do? Previously you spent every waking hour compulsively looking for sex. Now what will you do? Finding meaningful replacement activities is one of a recovering addict's hardest challenges, as it will not satisfy him to merely plunk himself down in front of the television set or serve him to veer in the direction of some new harmful obsession. One of the satisfactory things he can do is to use creating as his signature replacement strategy.

The Canadian painter Robert Genn explains: "Replacement 'units' can be tailor-made to the previous addiction. A cigarette, for example, burns down in about eight minutes. The idea is to make eight-minute poems, paintings, or whatever. These units can be repeated in about the same frequency and timing as the previous addiction. This is habit management and it can be a lot of fun. It's important not to give yourself time to think. A bad habit is simply replaced by a good one. Materials at hand are the only prerequisite—freshly squeezed paint, that sort of thing. This system is called CAR—Creative Addiction Replacement. It's a proactive way to keep the mind from the depressing stuff. Like pulling a cigarette out of a packet and lighting up, it requires an action without a lot of thought."

In order for this replacement strategy to work, you need to get into the kind of relationship to creating that allows you to move right to creating without a lot of resistance. If you have a lifetime habit of resistance and blockage and have done relatively little creating up to this point, then this replacement strategy will prove just another frustration. If, for instance, you've never found it easy to write every day, it is unlikely that you will suddenly find it easy to write for eight minutes many times a day. Still, the neatness and simplicity of the idea of replacing addiction-related behaviors with creativity-related behaviors may even help with your resistance and blockage. You are not asking yourself to produce great art but simply replacing an unwanted behavior with a wanted one.

You should approach these replacement stints with a certain cool attitude rather than with the white-hot passion that signals that you have put yourself in overdrive. In early recovery especially, care has to be taken to avoid obsessions, anxiety, and frustration. The line to walk here is delicate. You want to feel excited about your creative work—to feel otherwise is to court apathy and depression. At the same time, you don't want to push yourself in ways that court danger. The phrases "cool excitement" and "measured intensity" capture something of this idea: that there is a way to be that allows you to love your creative work while, at the same time, not racing yourself along so fast that you need the bottle, the pill, or the wager to come down. Let's take a look at how this intricate process played itself out in one artist's life.

The Case of Howard L.

Howard drank alcoholically from the age of sixteen until he was thirty-five. During that period he graduated from college, joined the Peace Corps, earned a PhD in urban planning, and worked for several years in a nonprofit organization as a project planner. From the outside, Howard's path made perfect sense. But to Howard it made no sense at all, since he could find no meaning in his work. What urban planning meant in his heart was the transformation of cities; what it meant in reality was collecting data, attending meetings, helping to configure minor legislation, and feeling endlessly restless and bored. In response—and for many other reasons, including what looked like a significant genetic propensity—he drank.

He hit bottom with a bar fight and a car wreck on the same night. The long road back started at that point. Howard began attending AA meetings and white-knuckling his sobriety. For the most part he managed not to drink, but his essential feelings did not change. He still felt empty, lonely, and worthless; he still got precious little satisfaction from his work; he still felt that he was mismanaging his life and misusing his gifts. He'd had such big dreams and such large goals, and here he was pushing paper and making no real difference. He doubted that he could maintain his sobriety if something essential at the level of meaning didn't change.

One day, just like that, but as the culmination of months of inner work, Howard surrendered to the fact that urban planning could never mean what he had hoped it would mean. He'd had some romantic, utopian notions about how cities could be transformed into shining citadels, and now he recognized to what extent that had been wishful, magical thinking. He also recognized how grandiose he had been, designating himself as someone who could single-handedly transform the world's cities. Continuing the work of recovery, he saw that he had two choices: to pursue urban planning exactly as it was, as relatively boring, routine, and highly political work that culminated in the occasional small success, or do something completely different with his life.

He acknowledged that early recovery was not the best time to initiate big life changes. At the same time, he could practically guarantee his relapse if he didn't address the twin issues of creativity and meaning. He needed to feel more creative and he needed more meaning in his life. He also needed to make a living, maintain stability, and not engage in new wishful thinking by romanticizing some other path. To his surprise, he discovered that thinking this way did not make him anxious or unhappy. It pleased him that he was trying to think with a clear head and wide-open eyes about his creative needs, his meaning-making needs, and his basic survival needs.

One night he had a dream about making fine cabinets. When he awoke, he realized that he wanted to work with his hands. His father, an alcoholic too, had fashioned beautiful furniture. Howard had always loved being in his father's workshop, watching his father make everything from cradles to rocking chairs there. He wondered if making furniture might prove meaningful enough to someone who had always had high intellectual ambitions and aspirations of saving the world. Could he scale down and be happy as a mere craftsman? At first it seemed like an unlikely possibility. But as the days passed he began to see that his old ideas of "meaningful" felt less valid. He began to feel certain that crafting beautiful furniture could serve his meaning needs, his creativity needs, and his recovery needs.

It took several years, but over time Howard made the movement from ambitious, egotistic, bored urban planner to humble, accomplished, content, and sought-after handcrafter of fine furniture. His new life even paved the way for an intimate relationship and, later, a family. As a young man, he thought he would create cities; as a mature man, he accepted that creating a chair or a bureau suited his personality, served his recovery, and filled his life with sufficient meaning. He had arrived at a grand but not grandiose destination, where the satisfactions were abundant, the recovery solid, and the creating an everyday reality.

CREATIVE-RECOVERY EXERCISES

1. Practice replacing one of your addictive behaviors with an "equal amount" of creating. First, think through what this will mean: for instance, are you going to replace every single urge to smoke with eight minutes of writing or painting or are you going to engage in creative replacement only a handful of times each day? Get a clear picture in mind; then begin to substitute creative stints for your addictive behaviors.
2. Mull over the phrases "cool excitement" and "measured intensity." Explain to yourself how they capture something important about the way you want to approach creating in recovery.

The Satisfaction of Creating

One of the centerpieces of a meaningful life for a creative person is creating. Creative people look to give life meaning by making meaning investments in writing, sculpting, composing, filmmaking, biological theorizing, inventing, or other engaging pursuits. They feel it in their bones that creating is like nothing else, that nothing matches it in terms of providing deep satisfaction and an outlet for their intellectual, existential, and spiritual needs. For the creative person, recovery would feel like a paltry thing if it did not include creating.

The need to create will feel like a crucial piece of your recovery puzzle. However, all the challenges that make creating difficult in the first place, some of which may have contributed to your addiction, remain. It follows that you will want to handle these challenges more effectively this time around. This time you will want to have much better anxiety-management tools in place. This time you will want to be much better aware of your self-talk and much better able to get a grip on your mind. This time you will want to feel confident that the challenges of the creative life that previously derailed you do not derail you again.

If you have aspirations to do excellent work and to make a career in the arts, a key to meaningful creating is choosing projects that actually prove meaningful to you. It will not serve your recovery process or your artistic life to pursue creative work that you yourself deem meaningless. This may mean that you end up choosing projects that are dangerous by virtue of the fact that they rev you into overdrive, put you in touch with uncomfortable feelings, or have relatively little commercial appeal and cause you frustrations when you market them. All the challenges of the creative life remain—but this time you get to deal with them with new skills, new attitudes, and the blessing of sobriety.

CREATIVE-RECOVERY EXERCISE

Describe to yourself how this time you will better manage the challenges and pressures of creating. Do a careful job of examining which aspects of the creative process and which elements of your creative nature you want to give special attention.

Creating in Recovery

People do manage to enter recovery and create regularly. The writer David Adams Richards describes his experience: "When I walked into that first AA meeting, people smiled at me and shook my hand. I hung around. But it wasn't easy. It wasn't easy at all. Sometimes it still isn't. It took months before I felt human, and three years before I was able to complete another book. But since then I have written ten more. Since then, by luck and by God, and though I have been sorely tempted, I have never taken another drink." No one, Richards included, is saying that it will be easy—only that it is a real possibility.

Mark, a painter, described his journey: "Smoking had become a big part of the process when I was painting. It made for a good excuse to stand back and look at the painting, and since I had a habit of getting too close and personal with my realistic paintings, it was a good strategy. In recovery from smoking I had to come up with a whole new way of seeing myself as an artist. I went through a long dry spell. During that time, there were countless canvases that never saw the light of day.

"Colors were muddied, drawings looked like an amateur had done them, and everything seemed unbalanced and without harmony. But I used those attempts to analyze my mental state. Eventually I broke through that difficult time and found myself going in new directions. Colors became brighter and the subject matter much more cheerful. I've never gone through a block like that since. Now I have the added knowledge that I can do anything I set my mind to."

In recovery, you may finally unleash your full creative nature. Miriam, an artist, states: "It wasn't until I kicked my addiction to alcohol and other substances that my creativity was unleashed—full throttle! I've learned that my creative energy is like a river; if it's not flowing, it overflows into harmful addictions. Two months after I put the cork in the bottle, I dragged out the sewing machine and started my creative journey. That was over sixteen years ago and my journey, which began with quilting, has led to jewelry making, writing, and painting—activities I had only dreamed of doing."

You will want to make a place for creating in your life—carefully, sanely, but surely. As a creative person, creating is at the heart of who you are. To work a recovery program that doesn't include creating is to walk a path without heart. Despite its attendant risks—risks that always accompany authentic living—creating is too important a part of your life to be ignored or abandoned. Creating was your birthright and is still your birthright, even as you steadfastly recover from an addiction. Here are the steps to take to make a place for creating in your recovery program.

1. Reaffirm that you are human

If you remember that you are entitled to make mistakes and messes, feel anxiety, do good work on some days and poor work on other days, and otherwise be human (as opposed to perfect), you will approach your creating in a good frame of mind and not jeopardize your recovery. As the writer Evelyn Lau explains: "The compulsions, the feelings of need and lack, are still there. I think now that these urges will stay with me for the rest of my life. But at least I no longer wake up every morning expecting to be perfect, then destroying myself if I am not." Be human, not perfect.

2. Analyze your exact risk factors

Which aspects of the creative process and the creative life cause you the kinds of anxiety, stress, and frustration that jeopardize recovery? This analysis may itself cause you anxiety, but it is an essential task. If your answer is "everything," then you have some fundamental work to do to change your relationship to the creative act and to put your recovery on a more solid footing. More likely, you will discover that only a few challenges really threaten you. Then you can plan how to handle those particular dangers.

For example Max, a sculptor, says: "Once I choose a project, I work with relatively little anxiety—in fact, the work soothes me. But choosing a project!—for those days I rush around like a madman, and during that crazy 'incubation' period I find myself very close to slipping." As Max did, do the work of noticing exactly where in the creative process your gravest risks are located.

3. Plan how to handle those risks

Once you identify your particular risk factors, think through how you will handle each one of those risks. For instance, Max recognized that he could safely skip twelve-step meetings while he was in the middle of fabricating a sculpture but that he had to attend meetings every day during his "crazy incubation period." Laura, a writer, describes her process: "At the beginning of a book, I have good manic energy and I stay buoyed up, usually for a few weeks. Then the hard work of the middle commences and I start to get down—sometimes a lot down. But the real problem comes as I approach the end—I have real trouble with ends. So I know that the second the thought pops into my head, 'How am I going to end this?' I had better get myself to a meeting. If the ending takes me thirty days, then I do thirty meetings—I know what's good for me!"

4. Work your program

The best guarantee that creating will not derail you is the ongoing mindful way you work your recovery program. For you, that might mean going to twelve-step meetings, seeing your therapist, reducing the stressors in your life, maintaining social support, keeping a watchful eye on your feelings and your self-talk, writing in your creative-recovery journal, or maintaining the mindfulness practice we described previously—or all of these and more.

As Giselle, an actress and dancer, explained, "I can deal with the grind of auditions, with the emotions of almost-but-not-quite getting parts, and with the stress of my day job, but only if I religiously work my program. I need to be steadfast in my recovery work, because if I let that slip, even for a day, I'm in real danger of losing everything. I don't ever want to go back to where I was just a few short years ago, drunk and suicidal. My program comes first."

If you are a creative person who is endeavoring to do excellent work in a particular medium and construct a career, you will need to break through resistance, overcome blocks, and deal with anxiety on a daily basis. The primary way you do this is by putting your creativity practice in place and attending to your creative needs in a regular, routine way first thing each morning.

In addition, you want to master a few anxiety-management techniques, learn self-coaching techniques for overcoming resistance and maintaining meaning, and become as expert as you can at negotiating the intricacies of the marketplace.

Remember that when we strive to do excellent work and endeavor to succeed in the marketplace, we produce anxieties that become risks to our recovery. The answer isn't to avoid attempting excellent work or to flee from marketplace encounters. The answer is to remain mindful of the risks involved, to deal with them in the ways we've been describing and in new ways that you learn for yourself as you work your recovery program, and to pledge to honor your creative nature and your creative aspirations. Creating is too important an aspect of a creative person's life to write off: what's required of you is that you pay attention to risk, maintain your recovery program, and create regularly and deeply.

Creative Exercises

This chapter's creative exercises focus on the need to create meaningfully while you mindfully recover from your addiction. You've been encouraged to utilize your natural need to create and use its healing power in your recovery. You've been invited to use creating itself as a replacement activity for addictive behaviors and to consciously practice the right balance between cool excitement and measured intensity as you create. Finally, you've been asked to assess the personal risks and triggers for relapse inherent in the various stages of your creative process and to make a relapse plan to minimize and manage them. You are invited once again to use your creative nature to explore these themes.

1. For the writer in you

Write a piece from the point of view of a creative person in recovery who is committed to his or her program but is also struggling with one element of creating, such as getting motivated, managing anxiety, or finding a project with meaning. How does your character resolve this dilemma?

What threats to his or her sobriety need attention? How do these get resolved? How does this apply to you?

2. For the visual artist in you

Construct a painting or a sculpture that illustrates your challenges to creating in recovery. How large or small, pliable or rigid a piece will this be? Notice your responses to your piece. Now do another piece illustrating your answers to those challenges.

3. For the dancer in you

Create a series of dance movements expressing the differences between creative apathy, manic pressure to create, cool excitement, and measured intensity. What do you notice about your attitude, your emotions, and how your body feels after the various movements? What does this tell you about your attitudes toward sober creating? Do these attitudes help or hurt your recovery?

4. For the scientist in you

Design a formula for utilizing the idea of creative addiction-replacement units in your life. First identify what areas of your work life require immediate attention in recovery. Be as precise as you can. What will your formula be at work? What will your formula be at home? Assess what personal or social obstacles would prevent you from implementing this. Design a solution.

5. For the dreamer in you

Imagine a world in which the healing power of creativity has become as powerful as the world's institutions, religions, and governments. How would you personally tap into that much power? Would you prefer to be under the influence of an addictive substance or behavior, or sober in recovery while using that power? Explain why.

Postscript

We hope you have continued to learn something useful about your relationship to your creative nature and how to use it in the service of your recovery as you read this chapter and did the exercises. We suggest you continue to pay attention to whatever sensations, visual images, memories, associations, emotions, thoughts, impulses, and judgments you make in response to these themes as you shift attention to the material in the next chapter, managing your early recovery.

PART THREE

Living

8 ◢◤ *Early Recovery*

Early recovery is a time of tasks and challenges. You've acknowledged that you have a problem. You've surrendered to the fact that the problem is large and real and must be met with more than wishful thinking and failed tactics. You've made certain decisions about the landscape of your recovery—whether you need an inpatient program to start, whether you'll use self-help groups as part of your recovery process, whether you'll try our creative-recovery program—and now you find yourself involved in a process that is completely unfamiliar to you as you deal with your obsessive thoughts and your painful feelings in new ways.

At the same time, you are trying to figure out where your creativity fits in. Can you still write or paint as you work your recovery program? Does that feel too difficult or too dangerous? Or have you discovered that you have been given a new lease on life with your creating? Gerard Way, lead singer of My Chemical Romance, says: "When I quit drinking and doing drugs, I was like, 'Is this going to make me softer? Is this going to make me lame?' And then I realized that mental illness, drug addiction, and liquor are all things that really hold you back as an artist." You may have trouble creating in the blinding light of sobriety, or you may experience a new burst of energy as you clear the cobwebs from your head.

Whichever is the case at first, over time you will discover that you have helped your creative life enormously.

Getting sober in early recovery involves a direct, no-nonsense emphasis on *what you do*. You need to establish effective structures, both internally and externally, to support abstinence (or, in the case of food and sex addictions, moderation). As you work your program in early recovery, you will need to build psychological, social, and behavioral bridges to carry you from addictive use to solid sobriety. In the early stages, a focus on the substance or behaviors dominates. In the later stages, that focus recedes and you shift your attention to life issues and creativity issues. First you focus on not using; then that focus shifts as your need to use lessens and other issues in your life demand attention. But you quickly return to a vigorous emphasis on not using when and if your recovery is threatened.

Establish Abstinence

Some people can establish abstinence without the structure and support of a formal treatment program and some can't. Whether you attend a treatment program or not, you will need to do two things: (1) continuously evaluate under what circumstances you are most vulnerable to using substances or acting out compulsively, and (2) protect your sobriety by modifying your environment, your activities, and your social interactions. This is especially important in early recovery when you are most susceptible to reverting to old behaviors and feeling triggered to use.

A common mistake that people in early recovery make is to assume that they can stay sober without having to make any substantial changes in their lives. This simply isn't the case. There are many changes that you must endeavor to make. For instance, you will want to consult with an addiction-medicine specialist to see if you can substitute nonaddictive medication for any addictive medication you may be currently taking. As a second example, if you are an alcoholic who smokes, you will want to try to quit smoking; research indicates that recovering alcoholics who continue to smoke cigarettes are at increased risk of relapsing on alcohol. Changes of this sort, as difficult as they may prove, are integral aspects of the recovery process.

The same is true if you have other cross-addictions. You will want to stop all of your compulsive, addictive behaviors, whether they involve gambling, starving and/or binge eating, compulsive Internet use, sexual acting out, or shopping. Stay accountable for *all* of these addictive behaviors as part of your overall plan for recovery. The more specific you can be about what constitutes your sobriety as you struggle with a package of cross-addictions, the more successful you will be overall. To repeat an earlier point: controlled moderation may be the right answer with respect to some substances and behaviors, but as a rule you should keep your focus on abstinence.

To maintain abstinence requires that you actively hold that intention and really aim to maintain that state. Here are seven practical ways you can maintain abstinence. You might want to turn each of these practical points into a personal mantra and post the seven mantras in a prominent place, to help you stay firm in your commitment.

1. Make a commitment to abstinence

Write that commitment down, say it out loud, and repeat it to yourself without doubt and without embarrassment. Be very clear that you have opted for abstinence. Assess whether you have left the door open for using or have really closed that door; and if your honest appraisal is that you are still keeping that door open a crack, visualize shutting it completely—and locking it shut. Your mantra: "I am committed to abstinence."

2. Clean out your immediate environment

Get rid of all the addictive substances and related paraphernalia in your home, car, and office and on your computer (that is, install firewalls to make it harder for you to order pills off the Internet, to gamble, to shop, to look at porn, or to act out in chat rooms). Get a supportive person to help you set up these firewalls if it is too triggering to do it by yourself—which it very often is. Your mantra: "I keep my environment clean."

3. Clean out your social circle

Cease making plans to hang out with anyone who is actively using substances or engaging in addictive behaviors. (If the person also happens to be your spouse, that is a more complicated matter.) Since many of these people have been in your life for years, you will have to tell them what you are doing and ask them for their support in keeping you sober. If they are active alcoholics or addicts themselves, they may try to discourage you from your recovery plan by denying or minimizing your need to change, rationalizing their own behavior, or accusing you of abandoning them. Don't fall for it! Remember that you don't need to make a decision about forever right now, only a decision about whether to see them while you're newly clean and sober. Your mantra: "I choose my friends mindfully."

4. Meet your friends in new places

Your friends who are not active addicts are likely to be willing to meet you in a coffee shop instead of a bar. If they are not willing to help you protect yourself, ask yourself what exactly you are getting out of the relationship. Put your recovery ahead of inconveniencing your friends or feeling embarrassed about asking for what you need. If you don't tell your friends what you're facing and don't ask for their support, you can't really expect them to know what to do to help you. Your mantra: "I let people know that I'm in recovery."

5. Stop hanging out in places where people are drinking and using

If you are chemically dependent, stay out of bars and nightclubs. If you are a compulsive gambler, stay out of casinos and off Internet gambling sites. Don't frequent people, places, and things that threaten your sobriety. When you can't avoid a slippery situation, make a plan beforehand as to how you will protect yourself. For instance, if you are a musician playing a gig in a bar, enlist support from one of your nonaddicted band mates and tell the bartender beforehand that you're not drinking and to bring you only soft drinks. Your mantra: "I avoid places that threaten my recovery."

6. Structure your time to support sobriety

Evaluate your patterns of drinking and using and implement activities that are incompatible with drinking or using whenever possible. For instance, if you are used to doing your art alone at home while you're smoking pot, arrange to go to your sober friend's studio and work beside her while your new habits are taking root. Your mantra: "My choices support my sobriety."

7. Maintain abstinence by creating

You always have the choice to work on your novel or to stroll over to the liquor cabinet. Get clear in your mind that abstinence allows for a richer creative life and more time for your creative activities and creative efforts.

Recognize that abstinence is not a loss or a trial but a gain and an opportunity: a real gain in creating time and an opportunity to finally realize your creative potential. Your mantra: "I can create now rather than use."

Increase Social Support

In his book *Creating Minds,* about the lives of famous creators in various fields, psychologist Howard Gardner discovered that over the course of their lives, his creative subjects used specific, ongoing support from others to help with their creative work. Those creative individuals—among them Freud, Einstein, Picasso, Stravinsky, T. S. Eliot, Martha Graham, and Gandhi—made use of confidants with whom they shared what they were trying to achieve, particularly at the time of a creative breakthrough.

Gardner describes the nature of this sort of confidant relationship as follows: "Under ideal circumstances, it ought to have two dimensions: an affective dimension, in which the creator is buoyed with unconditional support; and a cognitive dimension, where the supporter seeks to understand, and to provide useful feedback on, the nature of the breakthrough." Sometimes one person played both roles (as, for example, Braque served Picasso). At other times, these two roles were distributed among several people (in the way that Stravinsky turned to Nijinsky, Diaghilev, and others). We believe that your recovery also requires ongoing support in these two dimensions: in both the emotional sphere and the intellectual sphere.

It is better not to try a complete go-it-alone approach, even though we know that many people get sober without attending formal treatment programs, therapy, or self-help groups. We believe that the quality of your recovery is greatly enhanced by getting connected to others who understand what you are experiencing and can provide you with accountability and emotional and practical support. We strongly suggest that you establish significant and ongoing relationship support for your new life in sobriety.

According to the researchers Katie Witkiewitz and G. Alan Marlatt, "low levels of high-quality support" (that is, little support or sincere respect for sobriety) and "high levels of low-quality support" (that is, lots of lip service to staying sober but downplaying the real need for it) predict lapse incidents. Not only do you want the support of others, support that you must actively cultivate, but you want several supporters rather than just one, and you want to be in contact with them regularly and even frequently, rather than just sporadically when you feel lonely or at risk. These can be friends, family members, fellow self-help group members, recovery specialists, or your idiosyncratic mix of all of these: the important thing is that you get your team in place.

It may be difficult or awkward to change your social habits and increase your social support. Here are five ways to start. You might want to turn each of these practical points into a personal mantra and post the five of them in a prominent place, to help you stay firm in your commitment.

1. Seek out self-help meetings

Find out where the most accessible self-help group meetings near you are located. Try to attend a group specific to your addiction. Combine meetings if cross-addicted (for example, attend meetings of both Narcotics Anonymous and Sex Addicts Anonymous if you are using methamphetamine and also having unsafe sex with strangers). When you attend, don't keep secrets about your other addictive behaviors (although this doesn't mean that you have to share indiscriminately). Your mantra: "I go to meetings."

2. Ask for help when you need it

Get in the habit of reaching out to others regularly whether you think you need their support or not. You're less likely to call someone when you need help if you haven't been practicing calling your supporters regularly, when things have been going well. Along the same lines, not only make a list of safe people whom you'll call when you feel tempted to use (a list of at least three people) but also call them in the next twenty-four hours, just to check in and to report on how you're doing. If the first person on your list isn't available, call the next person and then the next. Keep trying. Your mantra: "I ask for the help I need."

3. Reach out to family and friends

Confide in family and friends—but only if they are respectful of your recovery and your recovery activities. Don't look for flowers at the hardware store—that is, don't expect real support from active alcoholics who are bound to minimize the problem, both yours and theirs. Be selective in where you reach out for support and be mindful of your own safety and sobriety as you connect with others. You don't want to isolate yourself, but you also don't want to reach out to people who are more likely to support your addiction than your sobriety. Your mantra: "I have allies among my friends and family."

4. Seek professional help

Consult an addiction-medicine physician if you have a history of severe withdrawal symptoms such as alcohol-related seizures or other detoxification complications related to alcohol or to substances like prescription pills (for example, benzodiazepines like Xanax or opiates like Vicodin). If you have a co-occurring medical problem that may at times require addictive substances, such as an upcoming surgery, serious dental work, or chronic pain, have your primary care physician consult with your addiction-medicine physician to best coordinate your treatment in recovery.

Ensure that you approach any such medical procedure from the vantage point of your recovery, not from the secretive, distorted thinking of your addict nature. Tell all of your doctors that you are in recovery and always stay current with the people in your support system. Don't isolate and don't keep secrets.

Seek an evaluation with a mental health professional who is knowledgeable about addictions if you have a history of repeated relapse or find that dealing with your emotions is a difficult matter and threatens your sobriety. If, for example, you regularly suffer from high levels of anxiety, depression, or other mood disorders; post-traumatic stress, bulimia, or some other serious ailment, seek professional help—especially if the symptoms are worsening. Unless the diagnosis predates the addiction, it is often difficult for a mental health professional to ascertain a person's mental health status until the patient has been sober for a minimum of two to six weeks, so keep that in mind. Reach out for additional support sooner rather than later.

Therapy is readily available and can strengthen your relapse-prevention plan by improving skills with emotion regulation, with tolerating frustration and other forms of distress, with self-assertiveness, with communication in general, and with anger management. For recovering people who cannot financially afford psychotherapy, try locating a low-cost clinic with a sliding scale based on financial need through county services, professional schools of psychology or medical schools, or your local psychological association.

Working the steps in one of the twelve-step programs with a sponsor can also offer practical support for dealing with emotions, resentments, and the challenges inherent in interpersonal relationships. The only cost to working the steps is your expenditure of time and energy. You can certainly afford that. Practice your mantra: "I seek out professional help."

5. Find support for your creative life

Creative people need support and advocates: writers need literary agents and publishers, painters need gallery owners and collectors, singers need voice teachers and accompanists, and so on. No artist who intends to have a career can go it alone. Just as you seek out support to maintain sobriety, you want to seek out supporters for your creative efforts so that you give yourself the chance to succeed. Success does not inoculate you against slips and relapses, but having no success is a daunting, depressing situation that can easily trigger addictive behaviors. So aim for success by seeking out marketplace advocates. Your mantra: "My creative efforts deserve support and advocacy."

Improve Self-Care

Improving how you take care of yourself physically, psychologically, socially, and existentially or spiritually is one of the most important areas of both early and ongoing recovery. Many addicted people were never taught how to take care of themselves effectively in the first place and hoped that mind-altering substances or behaviors would help them feel nurtured and comforted. Others started out with some self-care resources from their family of origin but lost their ability to access those resources as their addictions took over their lives. Whichever is true in your case, recovery offers you an opportunity to learn how to take care of your real self.

Self-care includes monitoring your moods, having good strategies in place for achieving balance, and learning home remedies for the everyday challenges of life—like taking a hot shower to quiet down racing emotions or driving out of the fog and finding some sun to help with a mild case of the blues. It involves rewarding yourself with appropriate treats, asking for what you want and what you need, and entering into satisfying, life-affirming relationships. It resembles the care lavished on a child by a loving parent: simple things like hot food, warm baths, gentle touches, and compassionate attention. You might want to turn each of the following four practical points into a personal mantra and post the four mantras in a prominent place, to help you stay firm in your commitment.

1. Focus your attention on today

People who scare themselves about the future generally end up feeling overwhelmed, deprived, or resentful, which can lead to relapse. While planning ahead can prove helpful or necessary in certain circumstances, practice staying in the here and now in early recovery and attending to what's right in front of you. In the twelve-step groups, this emphasis is echoed in the famous motto "One day at a time."

Focus on the things you can do something about rather than worry about things you can't control. Whether or not you use the concept of God in your recovery, you can utilize the wisdom of the Serenity Prayer: "God grant me the serenity to accept the things I cannot change, the courage to change the things I can, and the wisdom to know the difference." Your mantra: you can't really do any better than "One day at a time."

2. Practice positive self-talk

Practice a daily nonjudgmental attitude toward yourself and acknowledge your progress no matter how limited it may seem at the time, a practice that is very different from rationalizing away bad behavior. Similarly, practice supportive self-talk that strengthens your self-efficacy ("I can do this") and your commitment to recovery ("I really want to do this"). And don't forget to establish regular patterns of eating, sleeping, exercise, and relaxation.

Talk yourself into recovery behaviors (like reaching out or going to a meeting) and out of addict-type behaviors (like dropping into a bar just to have a look around or test yourself). Remember that the way you talk to yourself can be brought under your conscious control if you genuinely work at monitoring and managing your self-talk. Making a list of the negative consequences of your use can be a good resource to help with your self-talk when you find yourself struggling. Your mantra: "I am in charge of what I think."

3. Start daily recovery and creative tasks

Establish a daily practice of recovery activities—daily readings, a daily reaching out for support, daily attendance at a self-help meeting, the daily construction of a gratitude list, and so on. Similarly, establish a daily practice of meaning-making activities that support your authenticity and your creativity in sobriety, whether that's having some fun, being of service, making art, engaging in meditation or prayer, or genuinely connecting to others. Your mantra: "I practice recovery every day."

4. Really take care of your creative life

For a creative person, one of the most important aspects of self-care is caring for your creative life. It is in your heart to create regularly, deeply, and in ways that satisfy you, and if you aren't paying attention to those intentions, you won't feel complete even if the rest of your life is working well. You care for your creative life by maintaining a daily creativity practice, which keeps you focused on your creative efforts and helps you produce a body of work, and by maintaining a regular marketing practice, which helps promote marketplace success. Your mantra: "I take good care of my creative life."

Monitor Your Progress

It is up to you to keep track of your recovery. Others in your life may have a vested interest in your sobriety, but you are the only one who knows that you are suddenly sorely tempted, that you have not gone to a meeting in two months, or that, while you are still abstaining from drinking, you've relapsed with cigarettes.

Monitoring your progress means more than regularly appraising how close or how far you are from using. It means monitoring your progress with respect to all the work you intend to do in recovery: your self care work, your relational work, your work to make amends (if that is part of your program), your creative work, and so on. A recovery program is primarily about maintaining a clear, single-minded focus on not using, but it is also about making significant and even profound changes in attitude, in awareness, and in discipline. You need to monitor all of that.

You might want to turn each of the following six practical points into a personal mantra and post the six mantras in a prominent place, to help you stay firm in your commitment.

1. Faithfully keep your creative-recovery journal

Write in your creative-recovery journal at least on a daily basis and turn to it with a sharp eye rather than a lyrical bent. It is a place to really monitor your progress, which means noting difficulties that have arisen—and what you intend to do about them. If you find yourself writing in your creative-recovery journal "I am sorely tempted to drink," immediately add, "and because I am sorely tempted to drink, I am going to find a meeting as soon as I shut this journal." Your mantra: "I am keeping track of my recovery."

2. Carefully celebrate successes and regularly note achievements

You don't need to wait for ninety days or a year of sobriety to pat yourself on the back. In fact, if you get too concerned about reaching particular goals and too inflated and smug when you reach those goals, you tend to set yourself up for a lapse. Celebrate and note each day of sobriety, if only by smiling and giving yourself a pat on the back. Your mantra: "I celebrate my successes and achievements on a daily basis."

3. Make regularity a prime goal

In the twelve-step programs people are encouraged to do "90 in 90," that is, to attend ninety self-help meetings in ninety consecutive days. Just as you had a daily alcohol or drug habit or manifested a compulsive behavior on a daily basis, you will want to monitor your recovery and work your recovery program every day, without skipping even a single day. Whatever reason you put forward to miss a day of monitoring is unlikely to be a really good reason. Your mantra: "I work my recovery program every day."

4. Put as much energy into your recovery as you used to put into your addiction

When you work your program with energy and enthusiasm, your commitment is less likely to wane, and you will be stronger in the face of urges and temptations. Working your program with energy means getting to a meeting rather than thinking about getting to a meeting, making amends rather than thinking about making amends (if that is part of your program), and cracking through resistance and getting to your novel or your painting rather than thinking about creating. Your mantra: "I am passionate about my recovery!"

5. If your plan to stay sober isn't working, problem-solve what needs to change

Enlist the support of others in this process. Return to the basics, like attending ninety self-help meetings in ninety days, getting back on track with therapy or counseling, and keeping tabs on yourself in your creative-recovery journal. Try to identify what *exactly* isn't working—is it the pressure of a cross-addiction, a relationship problem, new stressors at work?—and do whatever is necessary to change the situation or reduce the stress. You mantra: "I can figure out what I need for my recovery."

6. If you are continuing to lapse (that is, briefly returning to using) or relapse (continuing to use), seek additional help

If you find that you are lapsing or relapsing, you must take action immediately. Your action might include joining a structured recovery program, daily attendance at self-help group meetings, or inpatient care. Don't allow yourself to think, "Well, maybe my recovery isn't *that* important"—it is! Since your addiction has multiple biological and emotional components, it can suck you back in if you give it even a small opening. The second you see that door opening, take action. Your mantra: "I respond immediately to threats to my recovery."

Your Relapse-Prevention Program

Relapse is a common but not a required aspect of recovery. We agree with the literature that relapse can provide an opportunity to learn from mistakes and strengthen recovery, but, to repeat, it isn't required that you relapse, nor is it some sort of singular blessing. It is simply a common feature of the recovery process and attests to the reality of the bondage that is addiction.

If you have a lapse, try to avoid all-or-nothing thinking that can set you up to keep using and can cause a relapse. An example of such thinking is to rationalize your secret desire to use by saying to yourself, "I've already blown it, so I might as well keep using." Rather than heading in the direction of relapse, go back over every element of your program and make new decisions about what needs strengthening, what needs changing, and what needs relearning. Remember: Many people with relapse histories eventually do develop sufficient recovery tools to stop them from relapsing. Make not relapsing a target goal.

Here are four practical suggestions to help you develop your relapse-prevention plan.

1. Become aware of triggers

Learn about common relapse triggers by reading recovery materials and talking to others. For example, taking a cue from the twelve-step programs, you might use the recovery acronym HALT to ask yourself if you are getting too Hungry, Angry, Lonely, or Tired, all of which are strong triggers to use. Another acronym is RID, which stands for Restless, Irritable, or Discontented. If you notice any of these triggers, take care of yourself accordingly, for instance by figuring out what's irritating you and deciding what you can do to change the situation or your reaction to the situation.

Identify your personal relapse triggers—the people, places, and things that tempt you to use. In addition, evaluate whether you are vulnerable to relapse because of any particular negative emotional states, interpersonal conflicts, social pressures, or specific triggers related to your creative nature or your creative life. Make sure to keep this list updated.

2. Create a plan for dealing with your triggers

Once you've identified your triggers, write out a specific plan to address each of them. A typical plan might include avoiding the slippery situation when you can, increasing immediate support so that you're not facing the situation alone if you can't avoid it, taking an alternate route to avoid exposure to a risky place, checking out your perceptions with a sober friend when you feel slighted by someone else's comments, and so on.

Be clear about who you'll contact depending on what situation or temptation you're facing. Make an extensive safe list and note in which situations you'll contact each person: this one if the problem is art related, that one if the problem is interpersonal, and so on. Check in with these people on a regular basis, even if no crisis is imminent, and make sure to keep your list updated.

3. Understand your definitions of "lapse" and "relapse"

If you are attempting controlled moderation for eating and/or sexual addiction, you will need to define "lapse" and "relapse" in terms that make sense given that your goal isn't abstinence. What will constitute out-of-control behavior with respect to your eating or your sexual activity? Just as you would if your goal were abstinence from alcohol or drugs, you want to identify triggers carefully and put a concrete plan in place to deal with triggers, temptations, lapses, and relapses.

4. Create a plan for dealing with a lapse or relapse

Create a plan that addresses what you'll do if you lapse. The lapse itself is one thing; using it as an excuse to relapse is another. Take your recovery seriously by creating a simple, sensible plan—including, for instance, calling someone on your safe list or going directly to a meeting—that you will institute immediately, as soon as you lapse.

Honoring the Process

Your creating, your addiction, and your recovery each exist in a particular context. The context is that you are not "done to," despite what may be powerful risk factors for addiction and your seeming powerlessness over a particular substance or behavior. Rather, you are an instrumental, creative, and powerful creature, powerful in a poignantly human way, able to get a grip on yourself and set yourself in the direction of hope, discipline, creative effort, and sobriety.

Manifesting that power may require inpatient treatment; attending hundreds of twelve-step meetings; changing your friends, your hangouts, and your celebrations; and engaging in an array of activities that make it seem as if you are essentially weak rather than essentially strong. If we were a stronger species, maybe we would never get addicted or maybe recovery could happen with a snap of our fingers. But we are not strong *like that*. We are strong in a humbling, amazing, and altogether human way. And because of that, we must approach life as a careful risk evaluator who keeps a watchful eye on all aspects of the recovery process.

We are not so strong that we can stand in a puddle in our bare feet and accept a lightning bolt. We are not so strong that we can ignore our biological and psychological nature. We are not so strong that we can act independently of our circumstances, our culture, and our human condition. But we are strong enough to take our contingency and our limitations into account—to fully and honestly account for our human reality and our shortcomings—and decide to be sober *and* creative. By making the effort, doing the work, and seeking help as necessary, these results are within your grasp. In that way you honor both the creative process and the recovery process.

Honoring the recovery process means noticing urges, identifying potential temptations, and staying alert to risks. It means *knowing* what it takes to maintain recovery (having a program) and *doing* what it takes to maintain recovery (working your program). It means putting recovery first. It means coming from the part of you that wants to live, that wants to create, and that wants the simple sanity of better health and fewer regrets. Above all, it means accepting as real your sneaky human penchant for inclining in the direction of a happy bondage.

Honoring the creative process means the following: If you are a novelist, you honor the creative process by writing your novel, strengthening and revising your novel, and advocating for your novel. At the same time, you honor the recovery process by dealing with the tremendous ups and downs of your writing life without benefit of your drug of choice, without succumbing to the lure of addiction, without opting for the happy bondage of an easy fix or an alley drama. Honoring the creative process and honoring the recovery process each take the same courage and the same forthright attention.

The poet Sheri-D Wilson, at that time in trembling, insecure recovery, recalled: "The Vancouver writers' festival had a special tribute to the honorable poet P. K. Page. The afternoon was filled with writers telling stories about their association with Page, most of which involved drinking antics. It wasn't until the poet herself took the stage that the magic was triggered. She read her poetry with the command of a lioness, never raising her voice, and a certain alchemy saturated the space. I thought I was going to explode on the spot, and I started to shake. As tears rained down, I felt like I needed a drink. There was too much intensity for my body to house. But why bring myself down with booze, I thought, why not experience the fullness of this? That's when I got it—the connection between poetry and love."

Your creative nature presents you with the possibility of love. Your addiction is primed to steal that possibility away with blandishments of unparalleled excitement, of a delicious loss of painful memories, of the startling ease of a fix. That addiction is no uninvited stranger, no unwelcome visitor—it is part of you. It is in the core of your brain and in the molecules of your body. The only way you can deal with something that insidious and internalized is by fiercely embracing reality and by tenaciously working your creative-recovery program.

Creative Exercises

Let's revisit the basics. You've learned that managing your early recovery will involve establishing abstinence, increasing your social support, improving your self-care, monitoring your progress, establishing a relapse-prevention plan, and honoring the recovery process. You will be simultaneously figuring out how your commitment to your creative nature and your commitment to your recovery can coexist and enhance each another. Learn more about these possibilities by giving the following exercises a whirl.

1. For the dancer in you

Create a routine that embodies establishing abstinence from an addictive substance or behavior and perform it for yourself. How elaborate or
simple do you wish to make this dance? Notice how difficult or effortless
this dance is to perform. Would including other dancers in your routine
change the routine or the feeling you have while performing it? What might
you learn about your own process of establishing abstinence from creating and performing this routine?

2. For the visual artist in you

Decorate a room in the spirit of recovery, then use that room as the primary place where you honor your recovery and sustain your recovery
awareness—where you write in your creative-recovery journal, maintain
your ongoing creativity practice, and maintain other recovery activities.

Notice how you feel about making that much room available for your
recovery. What internal or external obstacles did you face in creating that
space? How might you resolve them? Incorporate all of that experience
into your final room decor.

3. For the actor in you

Imagine yourself in a recovering addict's inner circle: as the addict's adult
child, parent, mate, friend, or peer. Play "support and acknowledgment"
from that person's point of view. Let the recovering addict know how
proud you are of him or her. Use this exercise to identify what you need
from the people in your support system and what you need to acknowledge to yourself about your progress in recovery. Make a plan to honor
those needs.

4. For the scientist in you

We have presented the basic elements of a creative-recovery program. Prepare the criteria for a personal-program evaluation. How will you measure the effectiveness of your program? Are there ways that you want or need to modify it so that it better fits your reality? Summarize your findings.

5. For the dreamer in you

Fantasize an art-filled, artful, art-committed, sober life in which you have all the recovery support you need and in which you take excellent care of yourself. Do not let go of that image! Use this image and the feelings that accompany it to help identify what is missing in your real life and where you'll plan to improve your social support and self-care as you establish and practice your creative-recovery program.

Postscript

After completing these exercises, mindfully observe what you're thinking and feeling about establishing and managing your early-recovery program in conjunction with your creativity practice. Continue to make notes in your creative-recovery journal. In the next chapter we give you a road map of what will follow as you manage your ongoing recovery.

9   *Ongoing Recovery*

Once you're sober and intent on staying that way, you've given yourself the opportunity to radically embrace and unleash the most complete version of yourself that you have ever known or imagined. Whereas your addiction promoted denial, avoidance, and isolation, your ongoing recovery requires you to stay connected to your true self, even when relating to others, and to be fully present whether you're alone, working in solitude, or having fun with a group of your friends. Should you decide to avoid this necessary growth and connection, you will remain at high risk for frustration, resentment, and relapse.

Many addicts have described the experience and promise of ongoing recovery. The writer Anne Lamott got sober in 1986 and shared her experience as a writer in recovery. She wrote: "My first sober book, *All New People,* wasn't a big success to the world, but it was a gigantic success to my soul because it was finally the book I wanted to write. My windows felt like they were washed and very clean, and I had a new perspective on the world. The last five books I've written, the work of a sober writer, are just huge gifts of my sobriety. I had a gift, a certain gift, not a huge gift, but a good gift, and it was being poisoned by alcohol and self-loathing and narcissism."

Learning to make authentic, healthy, and meaningful choices within these new realms of possibility is the work of ongoing recovery. You have embarked on something lifesaving and life changing, bringing with you into recovery all of your strengths, now made more manifest, and all of your weaknesses, now more truthfully acknowledged and better handled. At the same time, you are learning how to attend to your creativity needs and your creative efforts in new ways, more soberly, with more integrity, and with a real but modulated intensity that takes into account your commitment to recovery. This new life takes ongoing mindfulness, the acquisition of skills and strategies that support recovery, and a full-bodied attitude change in the direction of sobriety.

Your immediate goal is staying clean and sober. But ongoing recovery also requires second-order goals that support lifestyle balance, continued personal growth, and the healing of core problems from the past. These second-order recovery goals involve establishing, strengthening, consolidating, and integrating various aspects of self-awareness, self-acceptance, and self-responsibility into your daily life.

Self-awareness involves learning how to accurately identify and label core aspects of your genuine experience by utilizing cognitive, emotional, and physical cues. Actively listening in to your thoughts and corresponding self-talk is a good starting point, as most of us can access that by just focusing our attention on it. Once you start attending to your self-talk, we encourage you to become curious about where you originally learned some of these characteristic ways of thinking about yourself and others. For example, do you find yourself generally assuming your father's judgmental or suspicious stance toward others or toward yourself? How accurate or distorted are these views? Becoming aware of the cognitive climate you inhabit allows you to make necessary changes in ongoing recovery.

Knowing how to tune in to your physical sensations and emotions at mild and moderate levels of intensity (and before you are in high arousal and at the mercy of the more primitive lizard aspects of your brain) is the most basic building block of effective self-care and of healthy communication and intimacy with another. This also requires becoming more conscious of whatever defensive processes you learned that remove you from your genuine experiences, resulting in a false or adapted self, and interfere with your growth and integrity. Recovery necessitates identifying those powerful motivations, emotions, needs, and conflicts that have remained outside your conscious awareness in the past and have negatively influenced your behavior.

If you were not fortunate enough to grow up in an emotionally healthy family where it was safe for you to remain authentically self-aware, you will need to develop this skill in recovery. As with most aspects of self, this capacity needs to be developed experientially, in relationship to others. For those of you who did develop a capacity for self-awareness in childhood, your addiction has undoubtedly eroded your experience of it, though you will probably have a relatively easier time in ongoing recovery than someone who has to start from scratch identifying and discarding destructive patterns and building new constructive ones.

Whereas addiction typically results in your denying or ignoring your genuine needs, ongoing recovery provides you with the possibility of identifying your needs in real time. These needs may be physical, emotional, mental, creative, existential, or spiritual and include basic survival and safety needs, your need to receive attention and acceptance, your need to have fun and express yourself creatively, your need to experience nurturing and unconditional love, and more. Recognizing that you have these needs and becoming aware as quickly as possible that one of these needs has surfaced and must be addressed are important tasks in ongoing recovery.

Recognizing what you are thinking, feeling, and needing provides a solid basis for responding effectively to your internal cues and increases the probability of getting your ongoing needs met through direct rather than illusory means. As this internal picture of the you that you want to be comes increasingly into focus, your authentic identity, including your core values, life priorities, and dreams start providing a guiding internal map. You get to choose which parts of your early family dynamics and culture serve you now and which do not. For those who endured adverse childhood experiences and trauma, you get to resolve those traumas rather than run from them, and recover by separating and individuating as an autonomous adult whose sharpened self-awareness allows you to handle each of life's curves.

Self-awareness also involves observing the process of your recovery with honesty, patience, and compassion. It is always helpful to identify your primary, most essential feelings and separate them from any secondary feelings that can mask the primary ones. A typical example would be that you become angry (a secondary feeling) in response to feeling sad (a primary feeling). Making this distinction can help you empathize with and stay honest about your feelings and increases the probability of getting your actual needs met. Getting to the heart of the matter by increasing empathy for your primary feelings, rather than getting stuck in and perpetually responding to secondary feelings, is an important recovery skill.

In addition to self-awareness, also vital are self-acceptance and self-responsibility. Self-acceptance requires welcoming, or at least tolerating, the emotions and needs that you've now identified without shaming yourself for having them. If you can accept your feelings, you can learn to manage them better. If you can accept your needs, you are better able to get them met. If you can accept the whole range of your genuine human experience, your vulnerabilities and your strengths both, and accept them with grace and humility instead of avoidance and defensiveness, you can more easily get support and resolve problems. Your self-esteem begins to improve as you include your whole self, not split-off parts of yourself that are socially acceptable or intended to please people at the expense of your own integrity.

Empathy for your own position is crucial in being able to express yourself honestly to others. When people do not empathize with their own position, feelings are more likely to come out in distorted or even destructive ways. Instead of admitting that you feel vulnerable and are in need of reassurance from your partner, for example, you criticize and blame and shame her. You push her away instead of getting reassured and end up feeling worse instead of better. Of course, it is a different sort of problem if your partner can't tolerate your genuine feelings and, in response to your honesty, ignores your feelings or invalidates them. But first you must express them.

You must also take responsibility for your behaviors and for planning for and working on a healthy recovery. Self-responsibility involves establishing a safe, functional environment and identifying and handling your core recovery issues over time. Whereas some people have been painfully aware of their core psychological problems all along, others may not identify their latent psychological issues for many years into the recovery process. As your personal identity deepens over time and you become healthier and more mature, the story about your life and the role addiction played will evolve, offering greater understanding and opportunities for growth. It is your responsibility to keep pace with this evolution.

CREATIVE-RECOVERY JOURNAL QUESTIONS

1. In what ways would you expect your inner self-talk to change and improve as your time of recovery increases?
2. In your estimation, which of your feelings are primary and which secondary? Can you provide an example from your experience of responding to a secondary feeling while ignoring or denying the primary feeling underneath?
3. How might the picture of the you that you want to be change as your period of recovery increases? Do you have some predictions on that score?

CREATIVE-RECOVERY EXERCISES

1. Practice "busting yourself." Whenever you begin to move in the direction of unnecessary drama, whenever you allow an addiction trigger a foothold, whenever you veer away from your recovery program, jump out of your seat and cry, "Busted!" Then do the sober thing.
2. Describe in your own words what self-awareness, self-acceptance, and self-responsibility really entail. Think through which of these is likely to prove hardest for you and then outline a plan for dealing with this hard-core challenge. You might also try this exercise using your preferred medium, addressing the issues of self-awareness, self-acceptance, and self-responsibility through painting, dance, sculpture, performance art, or the like.

Core Recovery Issues

Following are several common ongoing recovery issues that are likely to rise up and confront you. In the resources section we provide references for those of you who want to explore these issues more fully; here we're presenting the headlines.

Problems with Self-Regulation

Self-regulation refers to your capacity (or lack of capacity) to manage crucial functions of the self—typically your emotions, self-esteem, and physical states. Ineffectual self-regulation of intense feelings and physical sensations is a major relapse trigger and a core issue for many in ongoing recovery. An example of ineffective self-regulation of emotion is when you lash out at someone before you even fully register that you feel hurt or angry, or you impulsively rush off to a bar and relapse because your novel just got criticized or rejected.

A dark joke in recovery circles is that when a not-yet-recovered alcoholic gets a flat tire, he calls the suicide hotline instead of a road service. Effective self-regulation involves identifying your angry (for example) feelings as they appear, whether they arrive as physical sensations or mental cognitions; pausing and reflecting on what is causing those feelings or thoughts (looking beyond the flat tire to the feeling that the whole world is out to get you); and mindfully considering your response options. When you effectively self-regulate, you pause to take the drama and sting out of situations, settle your nerves and your thoughts, and respond from a recovered, not an addicted, place.

As a sizable percentage of recovering people did not have healthy models for coping and conflict resolution in their families of origin, they also need to learn basic problem-solving skills and stress- and anger-management techniques. The same is true with respect to learning effective communication skills and understanding and utilizing the differences between *passive* strategies (often described as stuffing your feelings), *aggressive* strategies (that is, blowing up or bullying), and *assertive* strategies in which you confide appropriately and directly to those with whom you have a need to communicate.

When parents are attuned and respond accurately and empathically to their children's unique characteristics enough of the time, those children tend to develop a secure connection to their authentic experience. They have internalized the good care and attention they received from their caregivers and can apply it on their own. If you weren't this lucky, you need to learn how to do this now: how to be spontaneous, emotionally alive, self-assertive, appropriately entitled; how to self-soothe painful emotional states; and how to commit and to persevere. Improving self-regulation in ongoing recovery helps prevent relapse and allows you to continue the development of your true self that may have gotten derailed in childhood.

Problems with Interpersonal Relationships

Given that our most basic needs get met in relationship to others, identifying and correcting core interpersonal problems are essential tasks of ongoing recovery. For those addicted individuals who did not grow up in dysfunctional families, interpersonal problems tend to be limited to cleaning up the addiction-specific relationship wreckage. For the remaining majority, interpersonal problems existed prior to when the addiction took hold and almost certainly worsened as the addiction progressed. For these people, the task is not only to clean up the addiction-specific wreckage but also to overcome their inadequate parenting.

One important relationship issue is codependency. Initially described as coalcoholism in the 1970s, the pattern known since the 1980s as codependency generally refers to a chronic neglect of the true self in the service of a compulsive focus on controlling, taking care of, avoiding conflict with, and seeking approval from others. This pattern is understood to be a predictable adaptation to living with addictive, dysfunctional family dynamics of various stripes. Family dynamics that overtly or covertly stifle authentic expression and self-development, whether through neglect or intrusion, set the stage for codependency as people subvert their needs to preserve important relationships. Codependents often describe feeling anxious, angry, exhausted, empty and/or numb, and they regularly experience stress-related physical symptoms.

Recovery from codependency requires a refocusing of attention away from others and back onto the self. This is different from becoming *selfish,* which is an accusation codependents fear. Rather, it requires taking personal responsibility for getting your needs met and dealing with your feelings directly. This means differentiating the boundary between freely *caring* for others and *complying* with your perception of others' needs at your own expense. Breaking codependent patterns also requires learning to distinguish what is and is not under your personal control and staying on your own side of the street. When you are legitimately caring and know that you have a choice, you don't experience that aftertaste of self-righteous resentment or feel like a victim.

A second important issue is isolation, which is frequently caused by counterdependent feelings, that is, by a fear of losing your independence and a consequent refusal to succumb to the influence of others. This is often coupled with a chronic need to reject help even when you need it. Counterdependency is the mirror image of codependency and has similar roots in addictive family dynamics in which children are expected to caretake their parents or siblings. Isolation, whether or not it is caused by counterdependency, is a familiar by-product of active addiction and often maintains a life of its own after people become sober. Ongoing recovery requires that you identify and decrease your isolation and distinguish it from its soulful and nurturing counterpart, solitude, a state that is vital to the creative process.

A third important relationship issue and a familiar problem for many recovering addicts and alcoholics is the reenacting of abusive patterns from early childhood relationships in adult life. In an unconscious attempt to master the experience, or perhaps in the hope of having a better outcome this time, many people actively re-create situations that happened to them passively as recipients. One example of this trauma-bond phenomenon is when an adult child of an alcoholic repeatedly chooses as a relationship partner an unavailable or abusive alcoholic who helps her emotionally cocreate and re-create her dysfunctional childhood experience.

Because the emotions associated with these largely unconscious patterns are intense and deeply rooted, recovering people often mistake these connections as signifying true love. These relationships tend to reproduce patterns of high arousal with subsequent numbing that mimic many addictive systems. These trauma bonds often engender relapse triggers and need to be identified and healed in ongoing recovery. Genuine love involves healthy patterns of honesty, intimacy, comfort, and satisfaction and effective problem solving, not recurring pain and drama.

Resolving Trauma Related to Adverse Childhood Experiences

Identifying and healing trauma related to adverse childhood experiences involving loss, humiliation, helplessness, and/or danger are essential tasks for recovering alcoholics and addicts. The impact of trauma can vary widely depending upon how early, how severe, and/or how long the trauma continued, as well as according to what resources were available to help the victim reestablish safety and process it while it was occurring. But even if it occurred at the less severe end of the spectrum, unless the trauma is identified and healed its effects will play havoc with recovery.

Recognition of trauma issues may emerge at any time in the recovery process. Often trauma survivors have an intellectual memory of the experience but have disavowed the feelings associated with it, acting as though the trauma happened to someone else. Others do not even remember painful parts of their own stories. In early recovery, efforts are best focused on acknowledging and expressing feelings within a frame of relapse prevention, generally avoiding deep exploration unless the feelings are already causing distress. As sobriety becomes well established and overall safety increases, however, defenses against emotions become more flexible, denial softens, and the possibility of effectively dealing with and healing old wounds increases.

Resolving trauma issues in ongoing and long-term recovery best follows guidelines suggested by the author Judith Herman in her description of the stages of recovery from trauma: first you establish safety; then you remember, recognize, and reprocess what really happened; next you grieve and mourn; and finally you reconnect and integrate these experiences into other aspects of your life. As ongoing recovery from the addiction proceeds, the opportunity to recover from the trauma begins to present itself—and should be taken, as unresolved trauma constitutes a significant relapse trigger.

CREATIVE-RECOVERY JOURNAL QUESTIONS

1. What, in your own mind, are some keys to effective self-regulation? How would you describe the relationship between effective

self-regulation and being able to manifest your true or real self?
How would you describe the relationship between effective self-
regulation and getting your creative work done?

2. How would you describe your relationship issues in recovery?
Would you say that codependency is an issue for you? Would
you say that counterdependency is an issue for you?

3. Try to answer the following hypothetical question: say that a
person you know experienced some significant childhood trauma
that remains a frightening, humiliating, and half-unacknowledged
burden. When in his or her ongoing recovery, and under what
circumstances, would you think it safe or smart for the person
to begin to explore that trauma?

Troubles Creating

In the next chapter we address how to maintain a creative life at the same
time that you maintain a sober life. Here we want to highlight some of
the issues with respect to creating that are likely to arise in ongoing recovery. First, you will encounter the ordinary difficulties that go by such
names as resistance and blockage. Most people, even highly creative ones,
are resistant in a daily way to broaching the encounter with their creative
work and therefore put that encounter off until tomorrow—until weeks,
months, and sometimes years are lost. This is an enduring difficulty that
all creative people face and one that you will have to come to grips with
in ongoing recovery.

Second, you will have to deal with the realities of process. Creative
people, while they hope to do excellent work each time they create, will

see only a percentage of their creative work actually rise to the level of excellence. Several songs on your latest album may not be as interesting as the album's best songs. Your current series of paintings may never come to life and, in retrospect, may turn out to be a transitional phase as you move to a new way of rendering. Your third novel may not be as strong as your second. These are the realities of process and can't be avoided. What this means is that on a given day you may find yourself working on a novel that is turning out poorly; tomorrow you may find yourself in the same place, and a series of deeply discouraging days of this sort is a significant threat to your sobriety.

Third, you'll be confronted by craft issues as you struggle to shorten your wordy novel by a third, find the way to end your quiet screenplay so that the viewer feels satisfied, or get your mobile to move in the wind exactly the way you want it to move. Craft is a lifelong apprenticeship, especially for the ambitious creative person who is continually trying to stretch out of her comfort zone and create songs, paintings, or plays that maintain her own interest. Just as a carpenter may be stuck for the want of a nail, so a songwriter may be stuck for the want of a bridge to her current song, with all the attendant frustration and malaise that comes with being unceremoniously stuck.

Because resistance, blockage, process, and craft are enduring difficulties that confront every creative person, including the most sober ones, you will want to prepare yourself to face them by recognizing their reality and by accepting that your journey comes with exactly these challenges attached. Denial will not serve you here any better than it serves you with respect to your addictive tendencies. We list many resources to help you with these challenges in the resources section, and we continue this discussion in the next chapter.

Manifesting Your Creative Nature

You are unlikely to feel quite right if you don't manage to manifest your creative nature in recovery. Recovery itself is a blessing and a source of meaning, but it is not all the meaning that a creative person needs to make. Therefore it is vital that you remain adamant about creating. At the same time, it's important that you're careful with respect to creating so that you don't produce too much stress and jeopardize your recovery.

This may mean that you make choices of the following sort, especially in early recovery: you let go of the inner compulsion to get a new album out right away but continue performing at the venues you love; you put aside the novel that you've been wrestling with for two years and instead write a series of simpler but no less interesting or beautiful essays; you cut back on the number of craft shows that you attend, thereby reducing the pressure on yourself to continually produce new inventory.

It isn't that in every case you need to ratchet down your creative energy, creative drive, or productivity so as to guard your sobriety. Indeed, damping down your creativity to such an extent that you feel bored, empty, and existentially distressed is its own kind of danger. The goal is to walk a careful line, one that will become easier to walk with each day of sobriety—a line where you do your creative work while carefully monitoring the stresses that your creative work produces, stresses that can jeopardize recovery.

Here are seven practical suggestions to help you manifest your creative nature in recovery.

1. Maintain a daily plan and a schedule for your creative efforts; watch out for missed days; and make sure that you have a space dedicated to

your creative efforts, a private space where you can grow calm and lose yourself in the trance of creating. Don't assume that you need big blocks of time: the exercise of creating even for fifteen minutes every few hours will build your muscles.

2. Have a creative project in place to work on, one that you can name, commit to, and finish. You aren't really creating if you are only thinking about creating or if you are darting from project to project, leaving each unfinished. Calmly, without fanfare or drama, go through the whole creative process with each project: incubate it, start it, work on it, revise it, complete it, and if it is meant for the world, show it and attempt to sell it. Get in the habit of always having at least one meaningful creative project in front of you.

3. Keep an abundance model in mind, so that you don't overly attach to any one project and produce too much stress on yourself to get it right or too much pain if it turns out poorly. Picture a lifetime of work, rather than just a few isolated works, and by picturing that large bounty get in the habit of understanding that no single project defines you—or can hurt you. Learn to have excellent goals, ambitions, and dreams with respect to your creative projects while at the same time learning how to detach from outcomes, so that your ego (and your sobriety) won't be threatened if the project in front of you misfires.

4. Change at a visceral level, not just at an intellectual level, your relationship to mistakes, messes, and not knowing, growing more comfortable with all three in a deep way. Every creative person knows as an intellectual matter that she is bound to make some messes and some mistakes as she creates and that sometimes she will simply not know what to do next (until the knowledge comes to her, often in the doing). But most creative people viscerally hate this reality and want it to be otherwise:

they want to do only excellent work and to always know what happens next. Embrace the reality of mistakes, messes, and not knowing, as this is another example of necessary surrender.

5. Love your creative work even as it presents you with problems. There are so many challenges associated with creating that it's easy to fall into a negative, dissatisfied, unfulfilled relationship with your work, which produces stress, leads to incompletion, and ultimately threatens your sobriety. Counter this dynamic by consciously deciding that you will love your creative life, because you really do value it, and that you will love your current creative project, its flaws and shortcomings notwithstanding, because remaining affirmative affords you the best chance of completing it successfully.

6. Remember to pay attention to three distinct but related aspects of your creative life: your personality (including the ways you self-sabotage and prevent yourself from manifesting your potential), the creative work itself (and the ways that creative work presents real and often taxing challenges), and the world in which you find yourself (including the particular art marketplace in which you are trying to sell, if you are a career artist). All three require your attention; if you avoid facing any one of them, you will find yourself edging toward denial—a direction that threatens sobriety.

7. Make sure you have convinced yourself that what you are doing as a creative person matters, at the very least to you. If you do not believe that what you are doing matters, you will provoke a meaning crisis that can easily lead to existential depression and the urge to use. If you haven't convinced yourself yet that your creative efforts matter, have a serious conversation with yourself in which you air your doubts and fears and counter those doubts and fears with heartfelt reasons for advocating for your own creative life.

Preventing Relapse

The more you understand the nature of the relapse process, the better equipped you will be to prepare for and prevent having an initial lapse (a temporary return to use), or having a lapse turn into a full-blown relapse (a return to continued use). We've already indicated that relapse is a common part of the recovery process, but it is not a required part.

By the time someone has returned to drinking or using, it is generally the case that he or she had been heading in the wrong direction emotionally, cognitively, and/or behaviorally before relapsing. As the researchers Alan Marlatt and Judith Gordon put it: "A person who is headed for a relapse makes a number of mini-decisions over time, each of which brings the individual closer to the brink of the triggering high-risk situation. An example is the abstinent drinker who buys a bottle of sherry to take home, 'just in case a guest drops by.'"

Marlatt and his colleagues at the University of Washington have been studying relapse prevention for decades. They've identified common relapse triggers that account for a majority of the relapse episodes studied. These include intrapersonal factors such as negative emotional states (getting angry at a critic), negative physical states (being in pain as a dancer), positive emotional states (wanting to celebrate a book sale), testing personal control (seeing if you can drink socially now), and urges and temptations of all sorts.

These relapse triggers also include such interpersonal factors as conflicts (getting in a fight with your editor) and social pressure (being at a writing conference where everyone is drinking). Negative emotional states, social pressure from others (both the direct pressure of someone urging you to drink and the indirect pressure of watching others drink), and interpersonal conflict represent the most common relapse triggers.

You will also want to be mindful of the idiosyncratic triggers related to your specific subculture and to your creative nature. For example, artists in recovery often need to refute cultural stereotypes about addiction enhancing creativity or the artist's life requiring suffering. Musicians working in a bar atmosphere need to inoculate themselves against the exposure to alcohol and drugs. Every creative person needs to recognize those moments in the process—whether in the incubation phase, the working phase, the completing phase, or the selling phase—when anxiety rises and the desire to quell that anxiety turns your mind in the direction of using.

The long-term aftereffects of withdrawal often act as important relapse triggers. Acute withdrawal is generally short-lived, but postacute withdrawal lingers on. You may experience withdrawal symptoms for weeks, months, or even years after you stop drinking or using. Common symptoms of postacute withdrawal include depressed and volatile moods, reactivity and irritability, distractibility, difficulty concentrating or remembering, clumsiness, and sleep disruption. The best ways to deal with these symptoms are to identify them correctly when they are happening, learn how to manage your stress effectively, and maintain a strong program of self-care and creative recovery.

Donald, a writer, noticed that his relapse triggers changed as he increased his time in recovery. When he was actively drinking, virtually everything served as a trigger: not writing well, writing well and needing to celebrate, feeling alone in his writer's studio, feeling shy in the cafés and drinking to deal with his social awkwardness, and so on. In early recovery, he found it relatively easy not to drink in his studio but excruciatingly hard to enter a café or any of his former hangouts without wanting to drink. Over time he learned to manage this pressure by improving his social skills, making use of relaxation techniques, and growing more confident in social situations.

Then, as the years passed and his ongoing recovery proceeded apace, Donald noticed that the urge to drink would rear its head at three particular times: near the end of a book, when the outcome was in doubt; as he approached revising the book and had to look its goodness or badness in the eye; and when he had to deal with his literary agent, who always wanted the book to be different in some way. These three triggering moments followed one another in ominous procession, making the last three or four months of a book his danger time. Aware of this, he learned to pay special attention to his recovery needs during this precarious period by attending twelve-step meetings on a daily or nearly daily basis, regularly calling the angels on his safe list, and practicing his mindfulness meditation not once but twice a day.

All the following can prove relapse triggers for a creative person: getting your creative work criticized or rejected; experiencing difficulty with a current creative project and beginning to feel discouraged and defeated; experiencing few (or no) marketplace successes and beginning to feel that you have no chance of success; experiencing a great success and the mind-bending tumult that success and celebrity bring; suddenly believing that your creative work doesn't really matter, thereby opening your self up to an existential crisis; and feeling dry, uninspired, uncreative, and empty and fearing that this (probably) temporary state will this time prove permanent.

These are only a handful of the myriad triggers that are likely to threaten your recovery. The creative process is, by its very nature, arduous, daunting, and anxiety provoking, as is the creative life with its marketplace demands and its cycles of highs and lows. No magic bullet can make these realities vanish, and no artist, no matter how mature and sober, can handle every challenge with complete equanimity. What you must do is bravely, mindfully, and constantly work your recovery program, paying special attention both to your need to create and to the dangers that the creative process and the creative life inevitably bring. Let's look at these many issues as they arose in the life of one artist in ongoing recovery.

The Case of Graham

When Graham L. first came to consult with Susan, she recognized him as a celebrity musician from the late eighties and early nineties. He hailed from England, and his original post–new wave band enjoyed a respectable period of success around the world before the party ended. Susan remembered that she had one of the band's CDs, which she located among her collection when Graham became a client. She was pleased to find that some of the songs held up well. Graham's reputation preceded him, but Susan had learned long ago not to believe everything she read or heard. She was interested to hear his account of his life and his problems.

Graham was currently establishing himself as a music producer and was also the noncustodial father of a teenage son. He had relocated from Los Angeles to get a new start after getting a second DUI and to escape a series of unfortunate alcohol-related incidents. He described himself as burned-out on the music-business rat race in L.A. and came to individual therapy after completing a structured three-month outpatient chemical-dependency program in Napa Valley, close to the home of a sober long-time friend. He came to therapy with the following history.

Graham was raised in a working-class family in a London suburb with an alcoholic father, a depressed and self-absorbed mother, and an older brother. His parents bickered continuously, and periodically his father raged while drunk at whomever happened to be around. Graham's brother was his father's favorite, as they shared a certain macho gruffness and the tendency to bully others. Graham described himself as a sensitive and shy boy who felt that he didn't really fit in with his family or at school.

He was his mother's favorite and became her only confidant early on, to his own detriment. Graham's parents divorced when he was fourteen, and he went to live in another part of the city with his mother and brother. He saw his father infrequently and tried to stay out of his abusive brother's way as much as possible.

As he was tall for his age, Graham got away with drinking in pubs at fifteen and by sixteen was drinking habitually. He began listening to punk rock and new wave bands and learned to play guitar with some school-mates. Playing music and inhabiting the scene around it soon became his primary preoccupation, along with drinking. For the first time he felt that he fit in somewhere and could be comfortably himself. Alcohol helped him self-medicate the anxiety, chronic worrying, and self-doubts that had burdened him since childhood. He joined a band right out of high school and soon became a sought-after guitar player.

By the time Graham was twenty he was an up-and-coming celebrity in a popular band with a hit record in the United Kingdom and Europe. By the time he was twenty-two he was married and had a son and began touring the United States, resulting in long separations from his family. By then he was drinking daily and became increasingly distant from his wife even when he was home for extended periods. By twenty-five Graham had become a full-blown alcoholic. He experimented with various other drugs, including pot and speed, but generally preferred alcohol.

When he was about twenty-eight, Graham's anxiety began to escalate after a particularly stressful tour, a tour that brought with it intensified demands for publicity and numbing interactions with faceless strangers in city after city. He was becoming chronically dissatisfied with the di-rection of the band's music, and a couple of his bandmates' personalities were really starting to annoy him. He became increasingly isolated, and one of the road crew turned him on to Valium and Xanax, which he was soon washing down with vodka. Over the next six months this combination became part of his regular lifestyle.

In response to his wife's numerous attempts to reach out to him, Graham became more and more unavailable to her and to himself. Finally his wife gave up on the marriage and divorced him, taking their son with her. Thirty years old by this time, Graham was drinking and using heavily and felt spiritually numb, empty, anxious, and depressed. The newspapers carried the story of his hospitalization for "emotional exhaustion" after he accidentally overdosed on alcohol and Valium. Graham entered a twenty-eight-day chemical-dependency program in the United States, where he hoped he would be less recognizable and might be left alone.

Graham stayed clean and sober for about four years after going to residential treatment. He went to Alcoholics Anonymous meetings for the first two years after he returned to London but never followed the recommendations to get a sponsor and work the steps or continue with group therapy. He drifted away from all recovery activities and adopted a white-knuckle approach to sobriety. He was humiliated and ashamed of being an alcoholic and an addict and walled himself off, a process that increased the probability of his remaining miserable and returning to drink.

The band was stagnant and lost its major record deal. Graham was living off his savings and royalty checks. Eventually he went to work for a British record company as an A and R man, scouting new talent for the record company to sign. He hated it, especially the part where young musicians asked him, "When are you going to be famous again?"

Graham began smoking marijuana, rationalizing that using marijuana would be okay, since that wasn't his drug of choice. He told himself that he must not have been a real alcoholic, because he was able to quit for four years. He decided that the pills were his problem, and he'd be all right as long as he didn't use Valium. He relapsed on alcohol after about six months of smoking pot and was drinking daily by the end of the year. His only consolation was the pride he felt in staying off the pills.

He started playing music with some younger musicians and took them up on their offer to have him produce their debut record. He discovered that he really liked the process and was good at it. The record sold well and got good reviews from critics. Graham was happy to quit his job at the record company. He relocated to Los Angeles for his new career as a record producer. Doors of opportunity were opening and life was looking good, despite the alcoholic drinking.

Graham was thirty-five when he got his first DUI. He paid the fines, went to DUI classes, was inconvenienced by losing his driver's license for a while, and kept drinking. His production work went through alternate periods of feast and famine, as did his love life. He rarely had contact with his son. The old feeling of not making any meaningful connections seemed to be getting worse with every disappointing personal and professional relationship.

The blackouts started when Graham was forty. The following year he got into a minor automobile accident that was clearly his fault. Although he was fortunate that the woman and two children in the other car sustained only minor injuries, he got a second DUI. Because he had a previous record, he was facing serious legal consequences and hired an attorney. His attorney suggested he return to formal alcoholism treatment, as judges tended to look favorably on that. Although he was scared to fail again, Graham did not need convincing. He was demoralized and sick and tired of being sick and tired.

So it was that Graham found his way back to sobriety and the action stage of change. He was a reluctant participant when he first started in the structured outpatient program, but slowly he started to get it. He began to acknowledge fully the problem of his addiction, made the existential and spiritual step of embracing recovery and getting help, and began to employ his creative nature to help him experience a sober life as something meaningful. Instead of running the old "Graham's ego program of pride and isolation" that had failed him repeatedly, he allowed others to help him and started making significant changes in early recovery.

Even though external circumstances had propelled him to this point, this time Graham was able to choose recovery. Sobriety started to represent a want instead of a should. Borrowing a line from his favorite cult classic, *Dr. Strangelove*, Graham gave his story a subtitle: "How I Learned to Stop Worrying and Love My Sobriety." He completed his residential chemical-dependency program and, following the staff's recommendations for his aftercare, this time attended Alcoholics Anonymous regularly, got a sponsor, started working the steps, and continued in individual psychotherapy.

In his first year of sobriety, Graham focused on establishing a safe and supportive environment for his recovery by going to regular AA meetings and socializing with other sober people. With the help of his developing relationships with both Susan and his sponsor, he told the important people in his life, including the dentist and physician who had unknowingly enabled his access to pills in the past, that he was sober and in recovery. This process of honest disclosure, along with his ongoing step work, helped to mitigate the enormous shame and stigma he carried about being an alcoholic and having a history of relapsing.

Once Graham returned to producing music, he set clear boundaries with the musicians and recording engineers with whom he worked and kept the studio a substance-free zone. Instead of resuming the workaholic schedule that he used to pride himself on, he made an effort to limit the hours spent at work, eliminating the familiar pattern of all-nighters when he was finishing a record. He returned to playing guitar sober for the first time in years and started jamming with friends, despite deep-seated fears of being a mediocre musician when sober.

The more he played, the more relaxed he became about his playing. He started to improve, have fun, and get his chops back. He became increasingly respectful of his need for lifestyle balance—mentally, physically, socially, spiritually, and creatively—and could see the negative consequences that he experienced when he tried to override or ignore this need for balance.

Core recovery issues for Graham over the next four years of individual therapy included improving his capacity to identify and modulate his emotions and high anxiety states (that is, to self-regulate) and to risk expressing himself authentically. He began to identify and decrease the codependent and counterdependent patterns that had always led to disappointment and resentment in close relationships. His approach to dating changed from sexual search-and-destroy missions to taking time to know women as friends. He began the process of reconnecting with his estranged son by making amends to his son and to his son's mother, his ex-wife.

Later recovery work focused on family-of-origin issues related to his alcoholic father's abusive behavior and the deep shame he'd carried for years as a child of an alcoholic. As his recovery work progressed, Graham agreed to attend an ACA (Adult Children of Alcoholics) therapy group, where he could practice the new behaviors he was learning. There he began to better understand that a certain painful childhood dynamic, in which his mother's narcissistic need for him to take care of her emotions had alienated him from himself and from others, had left him with a desperate sense of chronic emptiness.

Graham also started the ongoing process of grieving childhood losses while simultaneously acknowledging his gratitude about his musical gifts and his current state of grace. With a daily recovery practice, a daily creativity practice, and a relapse-prevention plan fully established, Graham eventually left therapy, taking with him a newfound capacity for connection to himself and to others. Before he left, he was considering doing a reunion tour with his old band but wanted to see how the amends process went with them first. As many addicted artists in ongoing recovery do, Graham acknowledged that this sober time was by far the best time of his life: the sanest, the happiest, and also the most creative.

Ongoing recovery requires that you develop and stick to a new lifestyle that fully supports your health, creativity, and sobriety. This is no easy task, but by applying awareness, patience, and honest self-evaluation and by seeking outside help, creating a rich and rewarding life for yourself is a genuine possibility.

Creative Exercises

Use the following creative exercises to help strengthen the development of your self-awareness, self-acceptance, and self-responsibility in ongoing recovery. As you've seen, we encourage you to establish a daily recovery and creativity practice, to move toward lifestyle balance in all areas, to identify and heal your core recovery issues over time, and to fully nurture your personal and creative aspirations. Continue to mindfully identify and troubleshoot any threats to your sobriety, your authentic expression and growth, and your creative work in recovery. And don't forget to honor your recovery and cultivate gratitude for being a creative person today.

1. For the writer in you

Write a time-compressed short story that captures an hour in the life of an artist in ongoing recovery. What's working well? Are there vulnerabilities to relapse—psychologically, behaviorally, socially, environmentally, existentially, or spiritually? What part of the story felt the most satisfying to create for you as a writer? Why? Note any lessons for your own recovery or creative process.

2. For the musician in you

Make a creative-recovery-mix tape of original or cover songs that describes different stages of creative work: incubating it, starting it, working on it, revising it, finishing it, performing it, sharing it, and selling it. Do you have a favorite creative-process stage in recovery? Does that differ from when you were still drinking or using? See what part of the creative process is the easiest or most challenging for you in recovery. Plan to make that challenging stage more satisfying for yourself.

3. For the actor in you

Improvise a monologue in which a character describes how he or she lapsed and subsequently managed to get back on the wagon. Consider how your character's self-awareness, self-acceptance, and self-responsibility (or difficulties in these areas) figure in this story. What was missing from the character's program? What helped him or her regroup successfully? Consider the implications for yourself.

4. For the scientist in you

What markers distinguish early recovery from ongoing recovery? Fashion as comprehensive a list as you can. Now introduce the additional variable of creative work. How does this variable interact with your list for early recovery and ongoing recovery? What new challenges must you account for? Analyze how you will do this. Extrapolate from your analysis to your personal recovery.

5. For the dreamer in you

Dream up a wonderfully comprehensive picture of your creative aspirations in ongoing recovery. Describe your picture. Now imagine yourself fully engaged in your creativity while sober and achieving these aspirations while at the same time staying pleasantly detached from the outcome. How different is this from your actual relationship to your creative aspirations? What might help you move closer to your dream? How might you engage your recovery and creative nature to implement that?

Postscript

Engage in a few moments of reflection on the ideas of self-awareness, self-acceptance, and self-responsibility as you approach the last chapter of the book, where we continue our discussion of actively creating in recovery. Write down your observations in your creative-recovery journal so that you can refer back to them later on, to see yourself at different stages of the process. Mindfully accept whatever feelings and responses you're having and give yourself plenty of genuine credit for staying on this path of self-discovery.

10 ✎ Creating in Recovery

Active recovery provides the opportunity to do decades of creative work while sober. This may not seem like a blessing in the first months of sobriety or even in the first year or two, as you struggle to work your recovery program and wish you had a few drinks or a fix to help you with your current novel or painting. Ultimately though, as you find the way to access your emotions, go deep without fear, and tackle the challenges of the creative life without recourse to addictive substances or behaviors, you will discover that you have saved not only your life but your creativity as well.

Jeff Tweedy, founder and lead singer of the band Wilco, described his relief in learning that sobriety had only helped his creative life: "After I went through the process of being in the hospital and getting healthy, it was a huge anxiety for me to know if there was some kind of zero-sum game that would be played out in terms of Can I create without this tension, this anxiety within myself? When we first started recording and things began happening in the way they'd always happened, lyrics came the same way they had always come for me, songs just felt like, Wow, where did that song come from? Things started happening, and once it became apparent that things would be the way they'd always been, that I didn't have to trade health for creativity, it was an enormous relief."

That you are in active recovery doesn't mean that you won't experience depression, anxiety, emotional ups and downs, relationship difficulties, and the reappearance with a vengeance of shadowy parts of your personality. That you are in active recovery doesn't mean that it won't frustrate you to spend two years writing a screenplay that never comes alive, that it won't make you want to tear your hair out to have your excellent novel remaindered because of poor sales, or that it will inoculate you against doubts about your talent or your imaginative powers. Recovery may save you from drinking yourself to death, but it doesn't save you from life. Life—the good and the bad, the easy and the difficult—inexorably continues.

What recovery does provide is brilliant new possibilities. When asked to describe her experience in recovery seven years after she stopped drinking, the writer and columnist Caroline Knapp said: "For all the drama of being drunk and quitting drinking, for all the wrenching anguish of that split between the worlds of Before and After, sobriety is really about being a human—a plain old human at that, with plain old human struggles, joys and sorrows. Before: a person in a fog. After: just a person. I can choose to read or not read, deal or not deal, stay far away from that sea of emotion or plunge in headfirst. What sobriety guarantees, its unequivocal and daily blessing, is possibility."

Now you are obliged to face all of life sober. You have decided not to turn your anxiety into an eating disorder, not to mask your depression with stimulants, not to hide the truth from yourself about the real challenges of the creative life in an alcoholic haze. You have made it "harder" on yourself by opting for recovery and by bravely and mindfully removing the crutches and meaning substitutes that served you for so long. Now you've committed to having feelings rather than fleeing from them, seeing clearly rather than blinking, and standing up straight rather than ducking. This is honorable of you, smart of you, and healthy for you, but it is also keeps you awash in the cold spray of reality.

Before, your main challenge on a given day might have been scoring or dealing with your day job while drunk. Now your main challenge is likely to be one of the regular challenges that artists, sober or using, experience, such as actually getting to your creating, spending enough time there once you arrive, doing good creative work, and finding the wherewithal to effectively market your wares in a competitive marketplace. You may be sober, but you are no less an artist, with all that implies. You still have to show up, do the work, and live the life. That has never been easy for anyone and won't be easy for you just because you are in active recovery.

A central task for the artist in recovery is to face this truth straightforwardly and with as little fear as possible. You want to believe that you are equal to all of these challenges, especially the challenge of deeply creating, and are not hampered or hindered by having given up your crutch. As your recovery time grows, you want to grow with it into a confident person who is not scared to make significant creative messes and mistakes, who is not afraid to stand in front of a blank canvas completely sober, who is not afraid to access thoughts and feelings that were previously masked and held as taboo. The challenges may be real and hard, but you want to face them unafraid.

John, a painter, explained: "What I didn't want sobriety to mean was that I was supposed to live scared, unable to open up to the universe and let imagery pour through me for fear that, by being that open, I would lose control of my sober intentions and start drinking. I didn't want to become a white-knuckle painter, always afraid that big feelings, wild

intensity, and real passion were not allowed in my life and all that remained was tameness. That would be no life at all for an artist. By reminding myself of my intention not to be afraid, I finally became unafraid. Now
I can paint anything I want, any way I want. Of course, the result isn't always successful, but it feels wonderful to experience bravery and pride as
I stand before a blank canvas and know that I am actually present."

There are obvious tasks in recovery, such as attending self-help meetings, noticing triggers, making recovery a priority, and not using. There
are also many subtle tasks for a creative person, such as attempting creative work that suits your stage of recovery and your recovery needs. You
may need to hold off on an ambitious novel during your first months of
sobriety but tackle it a year later as you become aware that you're using
recovery as an excuse not to create. Similarly, it may be important for you
to paint explicit paintings of the abuse you received as a child, as that may
be exactly the work that your recovery, your therapy, and your art require,
but a time may come when painting those explicit paintings amounts to
a stuck place, an indulgence, and a way of not moving forward. These are
the sorts of challenges that will indubitably remain.

Among the challenges that are also likely to remain are anxiety, depression, and the last vestiges of unhealthy narcissism. Since anxiety is a
significant trigger and a threat to sobriety, and since anxiety is an integral
part of the creative process and the creative life—manifesting as stage
fright, everyday resistance to creating, generalized anxiety in the face of
marketplace interactions, and so on—you will want to calmly embrace
the fact that you will have anxiety to deal with for as long as you live. As
good as you get at reducing your experience of anxiety, some amount of
it will remain and must be managed. Each time you find yourself not
quite walking your walk—skipping days in the studio, not practicing your

instrument, doing more research for your current book than you need to do—you will want to stop and investigate whether anxiety might be the culprit.

Rose, a musician, tells us: "I don't actually feel anxious most of the time, so sometimes I let myself think that anxiety is no longer an issue for me. But I know better. I know that far too often I get to not feel anxious illegitimately, through avoidance. I act like I don't have a gig coming up, which allows me not to get anxious, but by acting that way I don't prepare properly and I don't inhabit the music properly. I am so practiced at dealing with anxiety through avoidance that I can avoid preparing even up to the last minute—and then I panic and perform at a low level.

"What I am learning is that it is vital that I accept my fears rather than try to dodge them. By accepting them, I actually end up reducing my experience of anxiety, because that allows me to become better prepared, more confident, and less defensive. I still have a lot of trouble accepting that it is better to acknowledge the elephant in the room than drape a tablecloth over it, but I am slowly getting better at being honest and less afraid of my fears."

You will probably also have to learn to deal with some amount of depression. Whether the grounds for your depression are biological, psychological, social, existential, spiritual, or some combination of these, the grounds tend to remain, and you are obliged to deal with your depression once again, although more efficiently and expeditiously this time because you are managing your life better. Recovery is neither an invitation to depression nor a depression cure; for the working artist who must face the fact that his last stroke ruined his current painting, that all of her books are now out of print, that he has never landed a dance role or an acting role as rich as the ones in his dreams, and so on, depression is bound to reappear in the picture.

Frank, a stage director, describes his experience, "At first I made no connection between my depression and my drug use. If anything, I thought the drugs helped. Then I began to think that the drugs were the cause of the depression and that if I could ever get clean that would take care of my depression. Now, after five years of recovery, I see that being clean, as great as that is, isn't the cure for everything. Clouds still come over me because the business is so hard, because trying to keep a small repertory theater alive is so hard, because always needing to raise money is so hard—so much of it is just plain hard. That wears on you; and in this city I'm surrounded by people making tons of money, which is crazy making in its own right. So I'm glad not to be using—but I'm not a happy camper."

If anxiety and depression remain edges in recovery, so does our tendency toward unhealthy narcissism and grandiosity. It makes perfect sense that we should take pride in our abilities, talents, ideas, efforts, and accomplishments. But this healthy narcissism is regularly accompanied by its ugly twin, unhealthy narcissism, an arrogant immaturity that causes otherwise decent creators to overvalue their creations, overinflate their opinions, and present an air of stubbornness, superiority, and privilege in their dealings with others. Sometimes this is manifested as dramas, tantrums, tirades, ultimatums, and flying glass; more often it appears in passive-aggressive ways, with an arch look here and a smile of veiled contempt there.

Richard, an actor, tells his story, "I left New York for Hollywood, became a full-blown alcoholic there and finally got into recovery, then returned to New York and did a lot of off-off-Broadway plays in places like Brooklyn and Queens. None of that really met my ego needs or my sense of the sort of career I was owed, and so I ended up in petty disagreements with everyone, just because I was so dissatisfied and so full of myself. I wasn't drinking, but I also wasn't very nice.

"Then my father got diagnosed with late-stage stomach cancer, and for some reason I finally 'got' the idea that the world didn't owe me a fantastic acting career. I'm actually no more satisfied than I was before and really completely unsure about what I should do to feel good about my life. But I have decided to be less of a jerk. That's now part of my recovery agenda: I want less jerkiness from me."

Jo, a Canadian writer, describes her biggest challenge: "After years of trying to chase down my unruly collection of addictions/distractions, the one that defies discipline and keeps running away from home is my Childish Self. This ornery and self-willed child seems to believe that she is entitled to be fed, comforted, and entertained 'just because.' She likes to nap in the middle of the afternoon, watch Elmer Fudd cartoons, and drink white pop with no bubbles from green bottles.

"She holds on to her belief that writing a great book and sucking her thumb go hand in hand, but if I dare to confront her about this, she stamps her little foot and runs away to her bedroom, where, with head buried under her covers, she reads endless stories about the interesting lives and adventures of other people. Whenever I bang on her locked door and ask her exactly when she is planning to write her book, she yells back at me in a sarcastic voice, 'Tomorrow is another day!'"

Our shadows, shortfalls, and addictive nature are hard, if not impossible, to eradicate completely. If your goals are to maintain your recovery, manifest your potential, create in a regular way, fashion a good career as a creative person, and make yourself proud by living an engaged, authentic, modulated, and mindful life, you have a lot to pay attention to each and every day. Your life isn't just about abstinence or just about succeeding as a novelist or painter. It is about spending today in a way that makes you proud, down to the details of showing up at your easel, showing up at a self-help meeting, and loving your loved ones—and spending tomorrow in the same way, and the day after that, too.

Florence, a singer, states, "We act as if we are simple creatures with nothing much going on inside of us, creatures who can 'just say no' to this and 'just say yes' to that. In fact, we re-create the whole universe within us, its tempests, its vendettas, its obsessions, its cosmic jokes, its ardor that causes stars to shine. It's amazing that creative people don't explode like a supernova, since so much is going on inside us.

"We may look quiet, sitting there, but we are a hurricane in waiting. Words like 'creativity,' 'recovery,' and 'addiction' can't do justice to the terrible, wonderful way we experience life. They may be useful words and they may help us communicate our shared experience, but they fall very short of capturing the way that a single life is an immense project, so very difficult, so very tumultuous, and sometimes so beautiful, too. We keep wanting life to finally be simple, but I don't think it ever will."

For creators, life is more like a tempest than a tranquil outing on a silvery pond. In addition, each creative discipline has its own risk factors, and a creator in recovery needs to monitor the special risks that accompany his or her métier. A writer can always write, but an actor must be hired; the actor has his recovery threatened by regular (and too much) unemployment. Conversely, when the actor is employed, he can get some of his relational needs met in the convivial theater world, while the writer's life is necessarily solitary, even if she contrives to write in the company of others. So the writer's everyday isolation can turn into alienation and loneliness that threaten her sobriety.

Similarly, all dancers and many musicians accumulate the kinds of chronic aches and pains that can threaten an addiction to painkillers. Performers—dancers and actors especially—are confronted by relentless pressure to maintain an unnatural and untenable thinness, a pressure that can easily lead to an eating disorder. Symphony conductors, movie directors, stage directors, trial lawyers, and lead surgeons can feel pressured to look powerful when in fact they feel only adequate; that kind of masquerade is its own risk factor for addiction. Serious challenges exist for all creative people, and then special challenges arise for creators in each discipline.

Nevertheless, you want to feel confident that as your recovery time grows, you will do an increasingly excellent job of meeting and mastering all of these challenges. So many of our most celebrated creators never mastered their urges, never entered sustained recovery, and finally died of their addiction that it would be folly to imagine that because you haven't had a drink in five years, you have transcended every issue. The itches run deep; the cells remember; the mind hasn't had its pleasure centers and its relic reflexes excised. You are still a tempest-tossed human being. But you can grow wise and adept, especially as you become expert at noticing how your addictive nature now wants to manifest itself—which is our next subject.

CREATIVE-RECOVERY EXERCISE

The rule with respect to creating in recovery is that the earlier or more insecure your recovery, the more you must focus on recovery and minimize the risks you take in your creative life, and the later and more secure your recovery, the more ambitious you can be in your creative life (while, of course, still maintaining a watchful eye on your recovery).

But this rule is bound to come with exceptions. Maybe you are both in early recovery and under contract for an ambitious book. Or maybe your recovery is shaky but you are offered a difficult but wonderful role in a new play. Must you cancel the contract or refuse the role for the sake of your recovery? No. But clearly you must pay special, daily attention to the risk you have added to your life by accepting the demands of writing that book or performing in that role.

Picture in your mind's eye how you will manage creative projects at each stage of the creative process, imagining that process as a continuum from early (and shaky) recovery to advanced (and solid) recovery. Draw a long line to represent that continuum and place markers along that road (like the anniversary of one year of sobriety, the anniversary of two years of sobriety, and so on), then jot down notes to yourself about what special care you will take at each stage to minimize the risk to recovery of undertaking ambitious creative projects.

Regularly revisit this matter as part of your ongoing recovery program by asking yourself the following two questions: "Is this creative project appropriate for my stage of recovery?" and "If this project feels risky but I still want to undertake it, what special care must I exercise as I undertake it?"

The New Face of Your Addictive Nature

The same addictive nature that supplied you with an alcohol addiction or an eating disorder is ready to keep you from doing your creative work in recovery. Maybe you don't drink now, but do you check your e-mail obsessively? Maybe you don't binge and purge now, but are you so obsessed with producing only perfect work that you can't get started? Listen to the following reports.

Shannon, a painter, identified her stumbling block: "In the spring, I was not satisfied with my creative productivity and I was looking for ways to increase it. What came to mind immediately was the computer and how I had become quite compulsive about checking my e-mail first thing in the morning. I realized that I would spend much more time with my e-mails than I had ever intended, feeling the need to reply right away, and by the end of that time, I would have lost a lot of momentum for creating.

"So I decided to switch my routine. I wanted to do the most important thing first, which for me is my art. I made a pact with myself not to turn on the computer until late morning or early afternoon and instead get up and create first thing. I would still check my e-mails, but by doing it later, I found that it didn't feel as important or take me as long. And by doing my art in the morning, I felt energized and empowered. I was putting my creativity first, and I felt more grounded and aligned with my purpose."

Sue, a painter, reported: "I've been away from home for five months caring for my elderly parents, my mom with cancer and my dad with Parkinson's and dementia. I've spent countless hours sitting in hospital rooms, waiting in doctors' offices, and waiting, waiting, waiting for my dear father to perform those activities of daily living that he can still do for himself. At first I filled the waiting time reading magazines and novels, which I thought was a fairly good use of my time and my brain, especially since I don't often have the luxury of long periods to read.

"Though I took my paints to the hospital on one occasion, I found it a bit too cumbersome and messy in a too-small room. At least that was my excuse. Then, as I became more aware of my father's decreasing cognitive function, I decided to exercise my brain with Sudoku. Therein lies my addiction. It is so easy to pick it up and work on a puzzle while waiting. But I finally became aware that I was hooked in an unhealthy way. It would be just as easy to carry a sketchbook, and so in my mother's final days, I took my sketchbook and captured images. I've resisted the Sudoku and picked up my paints again, working on a series about my mother and another series about my father's memory loss."

Sherri, also a painter, says: "I have experienced my own version of the 'distraction addictions,' and I think I've moved beyond them. Right now I'm working on recovering from a different 'addiction.' It's an 'addiction to potential' and the primary way I've kept myself from having to make creative choices. By keeping my paintings in my imagination only, I kept my disappointments with reality to a minimum. Finally, a couple of years ago, I committed to work daily. The anxiety was horrible, and a great deal of it came from being forced to make real choices.

"Beautiful paintings in my imagination became real messes on the easel. At first I could only begin paintings; then the practice of choosing took my work to the middle stages. Now I am beginning to finish work. I have learned the joy in making choices and in reacting to those decisions, and also the joy of letting go of beautiful visions. It is still all too easy to become stuck in the middle or later stages of a painting, but eventually even endings won't be as hard as they used to be. I still have disappointments, but there is no longer a black hole of disappointment in myself for not following through with my desire to create."

Our pull to experience the happy bondage of addictive behavior can manifest itself in a thousand ways, from the compulsive need to clean to the compulsive need to socialize, from the compulsive need to do just a little more research before writing our book to the compulsive need to get everything else done before we start on our painting. Peculiarly enough, and a testament to our very human ability to turn a silk purse into a sow's ear, we can transform creating itself into a kind of addiction, working manically rather than mindfully on creative projects and feeling as driven to create as we once felt driven to drink.

This last dynamic is naturally a special complication in a creator's life. A creator may love to paint, but what if she finds herself incapable of passing a blank canvas without needing to fill it up? A creator may love to write, but what if, out of compulsion, he finds himself recording every single one of his thoughts indiscriminately, thereby ending up with thousands of pages of undigested material? It is one thing to nurture productive obsessions and feel driven to produce your novel or your painting and a very different thing to use creating as a way to manage your anxiety, as if you were lighting up a cigarette or pouring yourself a drink.

Ralph, a well-known painter, describes the addictive nature of his painting: "I had the Picasso syndrome, most definitely. There were days I polished off three or four canvases in what had become my characteristic—and very easy for me—way, my signature geometric abstract style. And they sold. Galleries wanted them. Collectors wanted them. I was making a lot of money. And it was more than the money and the success that kept me at it—it was almost a mystical racing energy, it was as if I were on a brilliant sprint that nothing could interrupt, not people, not new ideas, not anything.

"But in the back of my mind I knew that I was becoming something like a performer or an entertainer, that I was doing something that was too easy and not really worth my time. I knew how not to drink; I didn't know how not to paint my signature paintings in my signature manic way. It took me a full three years to 'recover' as an artist, and for almost a year of that time I hardly painted at all—I abstained. But when I finally returned, I was able to paint with a new power, a new integrity, and with a kind of loving desire, as opposed to the manic desire that had been fueling me for years. Now I finish one or two paintings a week, rather than four a day, and without any craziness whatsoever."

We are not free of our addictive nature just because we have been in recovery for five years, ten years, twenty years, or more. It is part of the way we are built: that's why we had that two-pack-a-day cigarette habit or that lifelong misadventure with eating. The best we can do is to use our recovery awareness, our recovery tools, and our recovery program in ways that allow us to deal as effectively with a compulsion to check e-mails or play solitaire as with a compulsion to drink alcoholically. The compulsion may sneak up on us, but once we've spotted it we know what to do: treat it seriously with our full complement of recovery tools.

CREATIVE-RECOVERY JOURNAL QUESTIONS

1. How has your addictive nature played itself out in recovery? What has surprised you the most about the tenacity or trickiness of your addictive nature? At what point in the creative process are you most likely to be tormented by your addictive nature?
2. Which challenges of the creative life do you meet with an addictive response?

Creative Recovery and Authentic Living

Like many addicted artists, Sherry held to the belief that if she stopped drinking she would dry up as a writer. She understood that her third and fourth novels were not as good as her first and second ones, and that alerted her to the fact that something was wrong, but she chalked those less-than-stellar efforts up to other reasons. She argued that the first two novels employed settings she knew intimately, whereas the last two had ventured into unknown territory; that the first two relied on a conventional narrative style, whereas the last two were experimental; and so on. In her own mind, she didn't think that she was making excuses but only identifying where those novels had gone astray: and her drinking did not factor into the analysis.

Then she began coughing up blood, which scared her onto the road to recovery. She started going to AA, first sporadically and then fairly consistently; found a therapist who knew about addictions; entered very early recovery in a white-knuckle way; and began learning lessons from the process, lessons about lapses and incomplete surrender and the true hold of alcohol on her life. She found nothing much about the process easy and the pull to drink powerful and relentless. In fact it seemed as if the alcohol had indeed served to calm her, canalize her energy, and help her write, as she felt much more agitated and unproductive in her new sober state.

For a full year she found herself abandoning every writing project she began, usually after only a few days of sporadic and confused effort. She found it harder to sit at her computer, harder to go to that "writing place" inside her, harder to keep from being distracted by the hum of the refrigerator or the sounds of traffic. During this same time her second and third novels went out of print, demoralizing her further and precipitating a meaning crisis and a bout of depression.

She attempted to get help from her literary agent, wondering aloud to him about what she should do next and write next, but he replied absently and in clichés and showed no real interest in her plight or her future. She fired him—and then felt even worse, because she knew exactly how hard it was to acquire an agent, and now she had none. Part of her blamed everything on her sobriety: she had written better drunk, she'd had a better career drunk; wasn't sobriety the problem?

So she drank. For a while she drank harder than ever. Then she hit her lowest bottom, appearing drunk at a talk she was supposed to give in support of her fourth novel, a book that was limping along but still in print. She arrived so drunk that she could not function and could not miss the fact that she was an alcoholic. She left in humiliation without giving her talk and, for the first time, checked herself into short-term inpatient rehab. On a night that was among the worst of her life, she finally surrendered to the reality of her problem and committed to her recovery.

She began to count her blessings: that her drinking hadn't cost her her day job as a college teacher, that she was still young and healthy, that she had already actually written four novels and was a real writer, and that she still harbored hopes and dreams for her writing life that, to judge by the fact that she had been published four times, might not be unrealistic. She also began to understand how huge a part anxiety played in her need to drink, how uncomfortable she felt in social situations, and how frightened she often felt in front of the blank computer screen. She needed something to handle all of that anxiety—only now, she knew, it couldn't be alcohol.

She began a morning creativity practice and an evening meditation practice and instituted a real recovery program. Within a year she was settled enough to meet her demons and to begin a new novel, which, as the occasional novel does, came out whole and felt altogether successful. The first literary agent to whom she showed it offered to represent it, and an offer for publication followed shortly thereafter. Recognizing that excitement, like anxiety, acted as a drinking trigger for her, Sherry greeted this news in a quiet, understated way, making sure that her sobriety and her recovery would not be threatened by this excellent news.

Her next steps were not about writing but about living. In fact, she commenced writing a new novel very quickly, but she found that being in the world, holding herself open to relating, and confronting her fears about intimacy and life were the real tasks—and, it turned out, the real joys—of the moment. As her recovery progressed, so did the quality and amount of love in her life. She found herself becoming someone who was able to tolerate the foibles of other people, a change, she recognized, that amounted to her letting go of her stubborn sense of superiority. She was writing well, but more important, she was growing into a wise person.

We hope that your goal, as Sherry's became, is something grander than creative recovery, which is itself a grand goal. We hope that you choose as your goal authentic living. What constitutes an authentic life? It comprises a few simple principles: that you live ethically, passionately, and creatively; that you take responsibility for the meaning in your life; that you honor recovery and sobriety; and that you aim your life in the direction of personal integrity.

This is not a life that comes naturally. You must decide to live it and choose to live it. Many people don't. As a species, we are built to live any number of ways: anxiously, thoughtlessly, superstitiously, addictively, and so on. We can also live authentically, but that requires more effort. If you would like to live that way, then you must set off on a path defined not so much by what you want for yourself as by what you want from yourself. That is the key: what do you want from yourself?

Who are you intending to be? What are you backing? Do you want to put "acting with integrity" first or do you want to settle for lesser goals? Are you willing to accept the jarring nature of reality, an acceptance that demands lifelong courage and attention, or do you want to reduce your life to the equivalent of slogans? Do you want to take responsibility for the way you spend the next hour, or do you prefer to blame someone or something for stealing your life? Authentic living is about shouldering responsibility.

In order to make your ethical decisions now, when they must be made, you must be here right now and not live in the future or in the past, not defensively guard against now, not resist the rigors and responsibilities of now, but stand up right here, fully and bravely. This is the essence of authentic living and of creative recovery. Right now, you do not drink. Right now, you work on your novel. Right now, you notice your urges, your disinclinations to create, and your tendrils of anxiety. Right now you deal with each of them. In that way you maintain your sobriety, your creativity, and your authenticity.

Vincent van Gogh wrote, "If the storm within gets too loud, I take a glass too much to stun myself." The days of a glass too much are behind you, but the storms will come again. When they do, reach out for help and not the crack pipe; get drunk on light and not on scotch; turn to your recovery program and not to the poker table. At those times your life—and your creative life—hang in the balance.

Creative Exercises

We hope that you now see how your recovery can provide a personal platform for brilliant new possibilities, real choices, deeply authentic living, and a robust creativity while you continue to face the highs and lows of real life.

We reiterate that the general rule for creating in recovery is that the earlier or more insecure your recovery, the more you must protect your sobriety, maintain focus on recovery, and minimize the risks you take in your creative life; and the later and more secure your sobriety and recovery, the more ambitious you can be in your creative life while continuing to stay mindful of the risks. Life will sometimes demand that you veer from the safest path, but the stronger you've made your creative recovery program, the better equipped you will be to navigate the seen and unforeseen risks.

Bring everything you've learned to the following exercises.

1. For the writer in you

Write a "letter to a young artist" in which you explain what he or she should watch out for as a creative person prone to addictions. Read it aloud to yourself first, and then to another person who supports your recovery. What responses does your letter elicit? How would you suggest that this "young artist" protect himself or herself?

2. For the visual artist in you

From the viewpoint of a newly sober person, draw a mature, sober artist with a vibrant recovery. What would that newcomer in recovery see? Use this drawing to clarify what aspects of yourself as a person and as an artist you want to cultivate in recovery.

3. For the dancer in you

Create a dance that embodies authentic living in sobriety. Now add a movement that expresses the feeling of unencumbered creative flow. How do the two interact and influence each other? Pay attention to how you feel as you create this dance and perform it.

4. For the scientist in you

You have been chosen to lead a prestigious panel on addiction and the recovery process. What issues do you consider to be of paramount importance? Train your scientific eye on them, analyze them, and come up with solutions and conclusions. Share these conclusions now.

5. For the dreamer in you

Imagine that you have just celebrated your twenty-year-sobriety birthday at a twelve-step meeting. How do you imagine you would feel? How do you hope your life has evolved in recovery? What are you grateful for? How would you celebrate that success in a sober way? Use these responses as additional points of light to guide your recovery path.

Postscript

There you have it—the basics of creative recovery. We wish you decades of quality sobriety, grace and gratitude in recovery, and satisfying relationships with yourself and others as you fully realize your creative gifts.

Resources

Books

Alcoholics Anonymous World Services. *Alcoholics Anonymous.* 4th ed. New York: Alcoholics Anonymous World Services, 2001.

Arasteh, A. Reza. *Creativity in the Life Cycle: An Annotated Bibliography.* Leiden, Netherlands: E. J. Brill, 1968.

Azerrad, Michael. *Come as You Are: The Story of Nirvana.* New York: Doubleday, 1994.

Bateson, Gregory. *Steps to an Ecology of Mind.* New York: Ballantine Books, 1972.

Biglan, Anthony, Patricia A. Brennan, Sharon L. Foster, and Harold D. Holder. *Helping Adolescents at Risk: Prevention of Multiple Problem Behaviors.* New York: Guilford Press, 2004.

Boyd, Jenny. *Musicians in Tune.* New York: Fireside, 1992.

Bradshaw, John. *Healing the Shame That Binds You.* Deerfield Beach, Fla.: Health Communications, 1988.

Brown, Stephanie. *Treating the Alcoholic: A Developmental Model of Recovery.* New York: John Wiley and Sons, 1985.

Brown, Stephanie, and Virginia Lewis. *The Alcoholic Family in Recovery.* New York: Guilford Press, 1999.

Brown, Stephanie, and Irvin Yalom, eds. *Treating Alcoholism.* San Francisco: Jossey-Bass, 1995.

Cameron, Julia. *The Artist's Way.* Los Angeles: Tarcher, 1992.

Carnes, Patrick J. *The Betrayal Bond*. Deerfield Beach, Fla.: Health Communications, 1997.

———. "Certification in Sexual Addiction Workshop Manual": October 9–13, 2000.

———. *Don't Call It Love*. New York: Bantam Books, 1991.

———. *A Gentle Path through the Twelve Steps*. Center City, Minn.: Hazelden, 1993.

Coleman, Ray. *Survivor: The Authorized Biography of Eric Clapton*. London: Time Warner Books UK, 1993.

Crozier, Lorna, and Patrick Lane, eds. *Addicted: Notes from the Belly of the Beast*. Vancouver: Greystone Books, 2001.

Csikszentmihalyi, Mihaly. *Creativity*. New York: Harper Perennial, 1996.

———. *Flow: The Psychology of Optimal Experience*. New York: Quality Paperback Book Club, 1990.

Dardis, Tom. *The Thirsty Muse: Alcohol and the American Writer*. New York: Ticknor and Fields, 1989.

Denning, Patt. *Practicing Harm Reduction Psychotherapy: An Alternative Approach to Addictions*. New York: Guilford Press, 2000.

DiClemente, Carlo. *Addiction and Change: How Addictions Develop and Addicted People Recover*. New York: Guilford Press, 2006.

Ehrlich, Dimitri. *Inside the Music: Conversations with Contemporary Musicians about Spirituality, Creativity, and Consciousness*. Boston: Shambhala Publications, 1997.

Fanning, Patrick, and John Terence O'Neill. *The Addiction Workbook*. New York: New Harbinger Press, 1996.

Gardner, Howard. *Creating Minds*. New York: Basic Books, 1993.

Gorski, Terence, and Merlene Miller. *Staying Sober: A Guide for Relapse Prevention*. Independence, Mo.: Independence Press, 1986.

Hamill, Pete. *A Drinking Life: A Memoir*. New York: Back Bay Books, 1995.

Hayle, Aletha. *Opium and the Romantic Imagination*. Berkeley: University of California Press, 1968.

Heilman, Kenneth M. *Creativity and the Brain*. New York: Psychology Press, 2005.

Herman, Judith. *Trauma and Recovery.* New York: Basic Books, 1992.

Howard, Pierce J. *The Owner's Manual for the Brain: Everyday Applications from Mind-Brain Research.* 3rd ed. Austin, Tex.: Bard Press, 2006.

Inaba, Darryl S., and William E. Cohen. *Uppers, Downers, All Arounders.* 4th ed. Ashland, Ore.: CNS Publications, 2000.

Karen, Robert. *Becoming Attached: First Relationships and How They Shape Our Capacity to Love.* New York: Oxford University Press, 1998.

Kaskutas, Lee Ann, and Edward Oberste. *Making Alcoholics Anonymous Easier: A Manual.* Berkeley, Calif.: Alcohol Research Group, Public Health Institute, 2002.

Kendler, Kenneth S., and Carol A. Prescott. *Genes, Environment, and Psychopathology.* New York: Guilford Press, 2006.

Kirkland, Gelsey, with Greg Lawrence. *Dancing On My Grave.* New York: Berkeley Books, 1996.

Knapp, Caroline. *Drinking: A Love Story.* New York: Dial Press, 1997.

Leonard, Linda Schierse. *Witness to the Fire: Creativity and the Veil of Addiction.* Boston: Shambhala Publications, 1990.

Lewis, Thomas, Fari Amini, and Richard Lannon. *A General Theory of Love.* New York: Vintage Books, 2000.

LifeRing Press. *Presenting LifeRing: A Primer for Treatment Professionals.* 3rd ed. Oakland, Calif.: LifeRing Press, 2006.

Linehan, Marsha M. *Cognitive-Behavioral Treatment of Borderline Personality Disorder.* New York: Guilford Press, 1993.

———. "What Good Are Emotions?" Emotion Regulation Handout 2, Behavioral Tech Emotion Regulation Workshop, San Francisco, October 31–November 1, 2005.

Ludwig, Arnold. *The Price of Greatness: Resolving the Creativity and Madness Controversy.* New York: Guilford Press, 1995.

Maisel, Eric. *Coaching the Artist Within.* Novato, Calif.: New World Library, 2005.

———. *Creativity for Life.* Novato, Calif.: New World Library, 2007.

———. *Ten Zen Seconds.* Naperville, Ill.: Sourcebooks, 2007.

———. *The Van Gogh Blues.* Novato, Calif.: New World Library, 2007.

Margolis, Robert D., and Joan E. Zweben. *Treating Patients with Alcohol and Other Drug Problems: An Integrated Approach.* Washington, D.C.: American Psychological Association, 1998.

Marlatt, G. Alan, and Judith R. Gordon. *Relapse Prevention.* New York: Guilford Press, 1985.

Masterson, James F. *The Real Self: A Developmental, Self, and Object Relations Approach.* New York: Brunner/Mazel, 1985.

Mellody, Pia. *Facing Love Addiction: Giving Yourself the Power to Change the Way You Love.* San Francisco: HarperCollins, 1992.

Miller, Alice. *The Drama of the Gifted Child.* New York: HarperCollins, 1983.

———. *The Untouched Key: Tracing Childhood Trauma in Creativity and De-structiveness.* New York: Doubleday, 1990.

Miller, William R., and Kathleen M. Carroll, eds. *Rethinking Substance Abuse: What the Science Shows, and What We Should Do about It.* New York: Guilford Press, 2006.

Miller, William R., and Ricardo F. Munoz. *Controlling Your Drinking.* New York: Guilford Press, 2005.

Nakken, Craig. *The Addictive Personality.* St. Paul, Minn.: Hazelden, 1996.

Nicolaus, Martin. *How Was Your Week? Bringing People Together in Recovery the LifeRing Way; A Handbook.* Version 1.00. Oakland, Calif.: LifeRing Press, 2003.

———. *Recovery by Choice: Living and Enjoying Life Free of Alcohol and Drugs; A Workbook.* Reprint. Oakland, Calif.: LifeRing Press, 2006.

Raeburn, S. D. "Women and Eating Disorders." In *The Handbook of Addiction Treatment for Women: Theory and Practice,* edited by Shulamith Lala Ashenberg Straussner and Stephanie Brown, 127–53. San Francisco: Jossey-Bass, 2002.

Schore, Allan N. *Affect Regulation and the Repair of the Self.* New York: W. W. Norton, 2003.

Schuckit, Marc A. *Educating Yourself about Alcohol and Drugs: A People's Primer.* New York: Plenum Press, 1995.

Shane, Morton, Estelle Shane, and Mary Gales. *Intimate Attachments: Toward a New Self Psychology.* New York: Guilford Press, 1997.

Strauch, Barbara. *The Primal Teen.* New York: Doubleday, 2003.

Stromberg, Gary, and Jane Merrill. *The Harder They Fall: Celebrities Tell Their Real-Life Stories of Addiction and Recovery.* St. Paul, Minn.: Hazelden, 2005.

Vaillant, George E. *The Natural History of Alcoholism Revisited.* Cambridge, Mass.: Harvard University Press, 1995.

Washton, Arnold M., and Joan E. Zweben. *Treating Alcohol and Drug Problems in Psychotherapy Practice: Doing What Works.* New York: Guilford Press, 2006.

Whitfield, Charles L. *Healing the Child Within.* Deerfield Beach, Fla.: Health Communications, 1989.

Wile, Daniel B. *After the Fight: Using Your Disagreements to Build a Stronger Relationship.* New York: Guilford Press, 1993.

Wills, Geoff, and Cary L. Cooper. *Pressure Sensitive: Popular Musicians under Stress.* London: Sage Publications, 1988.

Zuckerman, Marvin. *Sensation Seeking and Risky Behavior.* Washington, D.C.: American Psychological Association, 2007.

Articles and Other Sources

Anda, R. F., and V. J. Felitti. "Adverse Childhood Experiences and Their Importance to Adult Health and Well-Being." *Congressional Briefing.* April 18, 2006.

Bellis, Mark A., Tom Hennell, Clare Lushey, Karen Hughes, Karen Tocque, and John R. Ashton. "Elvis to Eminem: Quantifying the Price of Fame through Early Mortality of European and North American Rock and Pop Stars." *Journal of Epidemiology and Community Health* 61 (2007): 896–901.

Brody, Jane E. "A Revolution at 50: Personal Health; Genes May Draw Your Road Map, but You Can Still Chart Your Course." *New York Times,* February 25, 2003, http://nytimes.com.

Carnes, Patrick J., Robert E. Murray, and Louis Charpentier. "Bargains with Chaos: Sex Addicts and Interaction Disorder." *Sexual Addiction and Compulsivity* 12 (2005): 79–120.

Davis, Diane Rae, and Golie G. Jansen. "Making Meaning of Alcoholics Anonymous for Social Workers: Myths, Metaphors, and Realities." *Social Work* 43, no. 2 (March 1998): 169–82.

Denizet-Lewis, Benoit. "An Anti-addiction Pill?" *New York Times Magazine,* June 25, 2006: 48–53.

Dube, S. R., V. J. Felitti, M. Dong, D. P. Chapman, W. H. Giles, and R. F. Anda. "Childhood Abuse, Neglect, and Household Dysfunction and the Risk of Illicit Drug Use: The Adverse Childhood Experiences Study." *Pediatrics* 111 (2003): 564–72.

Felitti, V. J. "The Origins of Addictions: Evidence from the Adverse Childhood Experiences Study." Published in Germany as "Ursprunge des Suchtverhaltens—Evidenzen aus einer Studie zu belastenden Kindheitserfahrungen." *Praxis der Kinderpsychologie und Kinderpsychiatrie* 52 (2003): 547–59.

Felitti, V. J., R. F. Anda, D. Nordenberg, D. F. Williamson, A. M. Spitz, V. Edwards, M. P. Koss, and J. S. Marks. "Relationship of Childhood Abuse and Household Dysfunction to Many of the Leading Causes of Death in Adults." *American Journal of Preventive Medicine* 14, no. 4 (1998): 245–58.

Goodman, Aviel. "Diagnosis and Treatment of Sexual Addiction." *Journal of Sex and Marital Therapy* 19, no. 3 (Fall 1993): 225–51.

Guisinger, Shan, and Sidney J. Blatt. "Individuality and Relatedness: Evolution of a Fundamental Dialectic." *American Psychologist* 49, no. 2 (February 1994): 104–11.

Knapp, Caroline. "After: Just a Person." *My Generation* (May–June 2001): 16–19.

Leshner, Alan L. "Addiction Is a Brain Disease, and It Matters." *Science* 278 (1997): 45–47.

Levine, Brian. "Brian Wilson: A Cork on the Ocean." *Scientific American Mind* (December 2005), 36–43.

Matano, Robert A., and Irvin D. Yalom. "Approaches to Chemical Dependency: Chemical Dependency and Interactive Group Therapy—a Synthesis." *International Journal of Group Psychotherapy* 41, no. 3 (1991): 269–93.

Pruett, K. D. "First Patrons: Parenting the Musician." *Medical Problems of Performing Artists* 19, no. 4 (2004): 154–59.

Raeburn, S. D. "Psychological Issues and Treatment Strategies in Popular Musicians: A Review, Part 1." *Medical Problems of Performing Artists* 14, no. 4 (December 1999): 171–79.

———. "Psychological Issues and Treatment Strategies in Popular Musicians:

A Review, Part 2." *Medical Problems of Performing Artists* 15, no. 1 (March 2000): 6–16.

Robinson, Terry E., and Kent C. Berridge. "Addiction." *Annual Review of Psychology* 54 (2003): 25–53.

Shaffer, Howard J., Debi A. LaPlante, Richard A. LaBrie, Rachel C. Kidman, Anthony N. Donato, and Michael V. Stanton. "Toward a Syndrome Model of Addiction: Multiple Expressions, Common Etiology." *Harvard Review of Psychiatry* 12 (2004): 367–74.

van der Kolk, Bessel A. "Clinical Implications of Neuroscience Research in PTSD." *Annals New York Academy of Sciences* (2007): 3–14.

Wills, Geoff I. "Forty Lives in the Bebop Business: Mental Health in a Group of Eminent Jazz Musicians." *British Journal of Psychiatry* 183, no. 3 (2003): 255–59.

Witkiewitz, Katie, and G. Alan Marlatt. "Relapse Prevention for Alcohol and Drug Problems: That Was Zen, This Is Tao." *American Psychologist* 59, no. 4 (May–June 2004): 224–35.

Whitfield, C. L. "Adverse Childhood Experiences and Trauma." *American Journal of Preventive Medicine* 14, no. 4 (1998): 361–64.

Wood, M., J. Read, R. Mitchell, and N. Brand. "Do Parents Still Matter? Parent and Peer Influences on Alcohol Involvement among Recent High School Graduates." *Psychology of Addictive Behaviors* 18, no. 1 (2004): 19–30.

Addiction Treatment Programs

Addiction treatment services range from nationally known, high-end private programs to local programs (some of which offer a sliding scale) funded through county health services or service organizations like the Salvation Army. Veterans of the U.S. armed forces may access addiction treatment services through their local Department of Veterans Affairs (Veterans Administration) programs. If you carry health insurance, your company often contracts with specific programs to which they will refer you. Some health maintenance organizations (HMOs) such as Kaiser Permanente offer their own addiction programs to their members.

We list some of the nationally known, well-established residential, extended-care, and regular outpatient treatment programs here. Local programs with a range of costs are also available in most cities. For low-cost services, we suggest you contact your local county or community health service or the Salvation Army for resources.

The Addictions Institute
445 Burgess Drive
Menlo Park, CA 94025
(650) 329-9779
www.stephaniebrownPhD.com

Beau Monde Programs
Newport Beach and Los Angeles, California
(800) 866-2948
www.beaumondeprograms.com

Betty Ford Center
P.O. Box 1560
Rancho Mirage, CA 92270
(800) 434-7365
www.bettyfordcenter.org

Cottonwood de Tucson
4110 West Sweetwater Drive
Tucson, AZ 85745
(800) 877-4520
www.cottonwooddetucson.com

Delancey Street Foundation
600 Embarcadero Street
San Francisco, CA 94107
(415) 957-9800
www.delanceystreetfoundation.com

Hazelden
Programs are offered in Minnesota, Chicago, New York, and Oregon
(866) 220-3091
www.hazelden.org

Life Healing Center
P.O. Box 6758
Santa Fe, NM 87502
(866) 806-7214
www.life-healing.com

The Meadows
1655 North Tegner Street
Wickenberg, AZ 85390
(800) 632-3697
(928) 684-3926
www.themeadows.org
www.mellodyhouse.com (codependency)
www.themeadowsdakota.com (extended care for sexual recovery)

Pine Grove Behavioral Health and Addictions Services
2255 Broadway Drive
P.O. Box 16389
Hattiesburg, MS 39402
(888) 574-4673
www.pinegrovetreatment.com

Promises Residential Treatment Centers
West Los Angeles and Malibu, California
(866) 390-2340
www.promises.com

Psychological Counseling Services
7530 E. Angus Drive
Scottsdale, AZ 85251
(480) 947-5739
http://pcsearle.com

The Salvation Army National Headquarters
615 Slaters Lane
P. O. Box 269
Alexandria, VA 22313
(The Salvation Army operates 120 Adult Rehabilitation Centers [ARCs] for substance dependence across the United States.)
www.salvationarmyusa.org

The Sexual Recovery Institute
822 S. Robertson Boulevard
Los Angeles, CA 90035
(310) 360-0130
www.sexualrecovery.com

Sierra Tucson
39580 S. Lago del Oro Parkway
Tucson, AZ 85739
(800) 842-4487
(866) 690-7241
www.sierratucson.com

Recovery Organizations and Web Sites

Al-Anon/Alateen
www.al-anon.alateen.org

Alcoholics Anonymous (AA)
www.alcoholics-anonymous.org

American Society of Addiction Medicine
www.asam.org

COSA Recovery
www.cosa-recovery.org

Debtors Anonymous (DA)
www.debtorsanonymous.org

Food Addicts in Recovery (FA)
www.foodaddictsanonymous.org

Gamblers Anonymous (GA)
www.gamblersanonymous.org

International Institute for Trauma and Addiction Professionals (IITAP)
P. O. Box 2112
Carefree, AZ 85377
(866) 575-6853
www.IITAP.com

LifeRing Secular Recovery
www.unhooked.com

Marijuana Anonymous (MA)
www.marijuana-anonymous.org

Matrix Institute on Addictions
www.matrixinstitute.org

MusiCares Musicians' Assistance Program
(888) 627-6271
www.musicares.com

Narcotics Anonymous (NA)
www.na.org

National Clearinghouse for Alcohol and Drug Information
www.health.org

National Council on Alcoholism and Drug Dependence
www.ncadd.org

National Council on Problem Gambling
216 G Street, Suite 200
Washington, DC
(800) 522-4700
www.ncpgambling.org

National Eating Disorders Association (NEDA)
603 Stewart Street, Suite 803
Seattle, WA 98101
(800) 931-2237
www.nationaleatingdisorders.org

National Institute on Alcohol Abuse and Alcoholism (NIAAA)
www.niaaa.nih.gov

National Institute on Drug Abuse (NIDA)
www.nida.nih.gov

Overeaters Anonymous (OA)
www.oa.org

S-Anon (12-step support group for family members of sex addicts)
www.sanon.org

Sex Addicts Anonymous (SAA)
www.sexaddictsanonymous.org

Society for the Advancement of Sexual Health (SASH)
P.O. Box 725544
Atlanta, GA 31139
(770) 541-9912
www.sash.net

Substance Abuse and Mental Health Services Administration (SAMHSA)
www.samhsa.gov

Women for Sobriety
www.womenforsobriety.org

Index

About the Authors

Eric Maisel

Eric Maisel, PhD, is the author of more than thirty books. He holds bachelor's degrees in philosophy and psychology, Master's degrees in creative writing and counseling, and a doctorate in counseling psychology. He is a California-licensed marriage and family therapist, a creativity coach and trainer of creativity coaches, a columnist for *Art Calendar Magazine,* provides regular segments for *Art of the Song Creativity Radio,* and hosts two shows on the Personal Life Media Network, *The Joy of Living Creatively and Your Purpose-Centered Life.* He lives in San Francisco.

Dr. Maisel is widely regarded as America's foremost creativity coach and has taught thousands of creative and performing artists how to meet the challenges of the creative life. His books include *Creativity for Life, Fearless Creating, The Van Gogh Blues* (a Books for a Better Life finalist), *Ten Zen Seconds, The Creativity Book, Coaching the Artist Within* (the first book on creativity coaching), *Toxic Criticism, Affirmations for Artists, A Writer's Paris, A Writer's San Francisco,* and many more.

In addition, Dr. Maisel is an active speaker and has participated in the Pike's Peak Writers Conference, the Jack London Writers Conference, the William Saroyan Writers Conference, the Oklahoma Federation of Writers Conference, the Romance Writers of America annual conference, and the Paris Writers Workshop, among others. Dr. Maisel also produces e-books available at his website, including *Becoming a Creativity Coach,* which details the art and practice of creativity coaching. You can visit him at http://ericmaisel.com or contact him at ericmaisel@hotmail.com.

Susan Raeburn

Susan Raeburn, PhD, is a licensed clinical psychologist in Berkeley, California with special interests in working with creative people. She has been in clinical practice doing psychotherapy and consultation for over twenty years with writers, artists, and musicians as well as writing about musicians' mental health. In addition to working with individuals, she has also worked with couples and bands.

Dr. Raeburn received a PhD in social-clinical psychology from the Wright Institute in Berkeley in 1984. Her doctoral dissertation was the first academic study of occupational stress and coping in professional rock musicians and was subsequently published in 1987. She did pre- and post-doctoral internships at Stanford University Medical Center in the Behavioral Medicine Clinic (1983–1986) and then worked as a staff psychologist and researcher at Stanford in both behavioral medicine and the Alcohol and Drug Treatment Center until 1992. In addition to private practice, she has been a part-time staff psychologist in the Chemical Dependency Services program at Kaiser Permanente in Walnut Creek since 1992. She is pleased to be a member of the Editorial Board of the journal, *Medical Problems of Performing Artists.*

Dr. Raeburn has presented papers and been active on panels at music industry conferences—including South by Southwest, North by Northwest, NARAS, the Future of Music Coalition, the Experience Music Project and E! Entertainment Television—on the subject of musician health issues and coping with the stresses and strains of the business. In addition to working with writers, artists, musicians, and bands, she continues to publish on musicians' health issues.

If you feel you would benefit from a consultation with Dr. Susan Raeburn or if you reside in the Bay Area and are seeking psychotherapy, feel free to e-mail her at sdr510@comcast.nct or telephone her at (510) 841-1820.